The Essential Guide to Leadership

D1132683

IN THIS SPECIAL ARTICLE COLLECTION:

Harvard Business Review

www.hbr.org

MANAGING YOURSELF

Traditional thinking pits work and the rest of our lives against each other. But taking smart steps to integrate work, home, community, and self will make you a more productive leader and a more fulfilled person.

Be a Better Leader, Have a Richer Life

by Stewart D. Friedman

Included with this full-text *Harvard Business Review* article:

Be a Better Leader, Have a Richer Life

The Idea in Brief

Life's a zero-sum game, right? The more you strive to win in one dimension (e.g., your work), the more the other three dimensions (your self, your home, and your community) must lose. Not according to Friedman. You don't have to make trade-offs among life's domains. Nor should you: trading off can leave you feeling exhausted, unfulfilled, or isolated. And it hurts the people you care about most.

To excel in all dimensions of life, use Friedman's **Total Leadership** process. First, articulate who and what matters most in your life. Then experiment with small changes that enhance your satisfaction and performance in *all four domains*. For example, exercising three mornings a week gives you more energy for work and im proves your self-esteem and health, which makes you a better parent and friend.

Friedman's research suggests that people who focus on the concept of Total Leadership have a 20%–39% increase in satisfaction in all life domains, and a 9% improvement in job performance—even while working shorter weeks.

The Idea in Practice

Total Leadership helps you mitigate a range of problems that stem from making trade-offs among the different dimensions of your life:

- Feeling **unfulfilled** because you're not doing what you love
- Feeling **inauthentic** because you're not acting according to your values
- Feeling **disconnected** from people who matter to you
- Feeling **exhausted** by trying to keep up with it all

To tackle such problems using Total Leadership, take these steps:

1. REFLECT

For each of the four domains of your life—work, home, community, and self, reflect on how important each is to you, how much time and energy you devote to each, and how satisfied you are in each. Are there discrepancies between what is important to you and how you spend your time and energy? What is your overall life satisfaction?

2. BRAINSTORM POSSIBILITIES

Based on the insights you've achieved during your four-way reflection, brainstorm a long list of small experiments that may help you move closer to greater satisfaction in all four domains. These are new ways of doing things that would carry minimal risk and let you see results quickly. For example:

- Turning off cell phones during family dinners could help you sharpen your focus on the people who matter most to you.
- Exercising several times a week could give you more energy

- Joining a club with coworkers could help you forge closer friendships with them.
- Preparing for the week ahead on Sunday evenings could help you sleep better and go into the new week refreshed.

3. CHOOSE EXPERIMENTS

Narrow the list of experiments you've brainstormed to the three most promising. They should:

- Improve your satisfaction and performance in all four dimensions of your life.
- Have effects viewed as positive by the people who matter to you in every dimension of your life.
- Be the most costly—in regret and missed opportunities—if you *don't* do them.
- Position you to practice skills you most want to develop and do more of what you *want* to be doing.

4. MEASURE PROGRESS

Develop a scorecard for each experiment you've chosen. For example:

Experiment: Exercise three mornings a week with spouse.

Life Dimension	Experiment's Goals	How I Will Measure Success	Implementation Steps
Work	Improved alertness and productivity	No caffeine to get through the day; more productive sales calls	• Get doctor's feedback on exercise plan. • Join gym. • Set alarm earlier on exercise days. • Tell coworkers, family, and friends about my plan, how I need their help, and how it will benefit them.
Home	Increased closeness with spouse	Fewer arguments with spouse	
Community	Greater strength to partic- ipate in athletic fundrais- ing events with friends	Three 10K fundraising walks completed by end of year	
Self	Improved self-esteem	Greater confidence	

Traditional thinking pits work and the rest of our lives against each other. But taking smart steps to integrate work, home, community, and self will make you a more productive leader and a more fulfilled person.

MANAGING YOURSELF

Be a Better Leader, Have a Richer Life

by Stewart D. Friedman

In my research and coaching work over the past two decades, I have met many people who feel unfulfilled, overwhelmed, or stagnant because they are forsaking performance in one or more aspects of their lives. They aren't bringing their leadership abilities to bear in all of life's domains—work, home, community, and self (mind, body, and spirit). Of course, there will always be some tension among the different roles we play. But, contrary to the common wisdom, there's no reason to assume that it's a zero-sum game. It makes more sense to pursue excellent performance as a leader in all four domains—achieving what I call "four-way wins"—not trading off one for another but finding mutual value among them.

This is the main idea in a program called Total Leadership that I teach at the Wharton School and at companies and workshops around the world. "Total" because it's about the whole person and "Leadership" because it's about creating sustainable change to benefit not just you but the most important people around you.

Scoring four-way wins starts by taking a clear view of what you want from and can contribute to each domain of your life, now and in the future, with thoughtful consideration of the people who matter most to you and the expectations you have for one another. This is followed by systematically designing and implementing carefully crafted experiments—doing something new for a short period to see how it affects all four domains. If an experiment doesn't work out, you stop or adjust, and little is lost. If it does work out, it's a small win; over time these add up so that your overall efforts are focused increasingly on what and who matter most. Either way, you learn more about how to lead in all parts of your life.

This process doesn't require inordinate risk. On the contrary, it works because it entails realistic expectations, short-term changes that are in your control, and the explicit support of those around you. Take, for instance, Kenneth Chen, a manager I met at a workshop in 2005. (All names in this article are pseudonyms.) His professional goal was to become CEO, but he had other goals as well, which on the face of it might have appeared conflicting. He had recently moved to Philadelphia and wanted to get more involved with his community. He also wished to strengthen bonds with his family. To further all of these goals, he decided to join a city-based community board, which would not only allow him to hone his leadership skills (in support of his professional goal) but also have benefits in the family domain. It would give him more in common with his sister, a teacher who gave back to the community every day, and he hoped his fiancée would participate as well, enabling them to do something together for the greater good. He would feel more spiritually alive and this, in turn, would increase his self-confidence at work.

Now, about three years later, he reports that he is not only on a community board with his fiancée but also on the formal succession track for CEO. He's a better leader in all aspects of his life because he is acting in ways that are more consistent with his values. He is creatively enhancing his performance in all domains of his life and leading others to improve their performance by encouraging them to better integrate the different parts of their lives, too.

Kenneth is not alone. Workshop participants assess themselves at the beginning and the end of the program, and they consistently report improvements in their effectiveness, as well as a greater sense of harmony among the once-competing domains of their lives. In a study over a four-month period of more than 300 business professionals (whose average age was about 35), their *satisfaction* increased by an average of 20% in their work lives, 28% in their home lives, and 31% in their community lives. Perhaps most significant, their satisfaction in the domain of the self—their physical and emotional health and their intellectual and spiritual growth—increased by 39%. But they also reported that their *performance* improved: at work (by 9%), at home (15%), in the community (12%), and personally (25%). Paradoxically, these gains were made even as participants spent less time on work and more on other aspects of their lives. They're working smarter—and they're more focused, passionate, and committed to what they're doing.

While hundreds of leaders at all levels go through this program every year, you don't need a workshop to identify worthwhile experiments. The process is pretty straightforward, though not simple. In the sections that follow, I will give you an overview of the process and take you through the basics of designing and implementing experiments to produce four-way wins.

The Total Leadership Process

The Total Leadership concept rests on three principles:

• Be real: Act with authenticity by clarifying what's important.

• Be whole: Act with integrity by respecting the whole person.

• Be innovative: Act with creativity by experimenting with how things get done.

You begin the process by thinking, writing, and talking with peer coaches to identify your core values, your leadership vision, and the current alignment of your actions and values—clarifying what's important. Peer coaching is enormously valuable, at this stage and throughout, because an outside perspective provides a sounding board for your ideas, challenges you, gives you a fresh way to see the possibilities for innovation, and helps hold you accountable to your commitments.

You then identify the most important people—"key stakeholders"—in all domains and the performance expectations you have of one another. Then you talk with them: If you're like most participants, you'll be surprised to find that what, and how much, your key stakeholders actually need from you is different from, and less than, what you thought beforehand.

These insights create opportunities for you to focus your attention more intelligently, spurring innovative action. Now, with a firmer grounding in what's most important, and a more complete picture of your inner circle, you begin to see new ways of making life better, not just for you but for the people around you.

The next step is to design experiments and then try them out during a controlled period of time. The best experiments are changes that your stakeholders wish for as much as, if not more than, you do.

Designing Experiments

To pursue a four-way win means to produce a

Stewart D. Friedman (friedman@wharton.upenn.edu) is Practice Professor of Management at the University of Pennsylvania's Wharton School in Philadelphia. He is the founding director of Wharton's Leadership Program and of its Work/Life Integration Project, and the former head of Ford Motor's Leadership Development Center. He is the author of numerous books and articles on leadership development, work/life integration, and the dynamics of change, including *Total Leadership: Be a Better Leader, Have a Richer Life*, forthcoming from Harvard Business Press.

change intended to fulfill multiple goals that benefit each and every domain of your life. In the domain of work, typical goals for an experiment can be captured under these broad headings: taking advantage of new opportunities for increasing productivity, reducing hidden costs, and improving the work environment. Goals for home and community tend to revolve around improving relationships and contributing more to society. For the self, it's usually about improving health and finding greater meaning in life.

As you think through the goals for your experiment, keep in mind the interests and opinions of your key stakeholders and anyone else who might be affected by the changes you are envisioning. In exploring the idea of joining a community board, for instance, Kenneth Chen sought advice from his boss, who had served on many boards, and also from the company's charitable director and the vice president of talent. In this way, he got their support. His employers could see how his participation on a board would benefit the company by developing Kenneth's leadership skills and his social network.

Some experiments benefit only a single domain directly while having indirect benefits in the others. For example, setting aside three mornings a week to exercise improves your health directly but may indirectly give you more energy for your work and raise your self-esteem, which in turn might make you a better father and friend. Other activities—such as running a half-marathon with your kids to raise funds for a charity sponsored by your company—occur in, and directly benefit, all four domains simultaneously. Whether the benefits are direct or indirect, achieving a four-way win is the goal. That's what makes the changes sustainable: Everyone benefits. The expected gains need not accrue until sometime in the future, so keep in mind that some benefits may not be obvious—far-off career advancements, for instance, or a contact who might ultimately offer valuable connections.

Identify possibilities. Open your mind to what's possible and try to think of as many potential experiments as you can, describing in a sentence or two what you would do in each. This is a time to let your imagination run free. Don't worry about all the potential obstacles at this point.

At first blush, conceiving of experiments that produce benefits for all the different realms may seem a formidable task. After all, if it were easy, people wouldn't be feeling so much tension between work and the rest of their lives. But I've found that most people realize it's not that hard once they approach the challenge systematically. And, like a puzzle, it can be fun, especially if you keep in mind that experiments must fit your particular circumstances. Experiments can and do take myriad forms. But having sifted through hundreds of experiment designs, my research team and I have found that they tend to fall into nine general types. Use the nine categories described in the exhibit "How Can I Design an Experiment to Improve All Domains of My Life?" to organize your thinking.

One category of experiment involves changes in where and when work gets done. One workshop participant, a sales director for a global cement producer, tried working online from his local public library one day a week to free himself from his very long commute. This was a break from a company culture that didn't traditionally support employees working remotely, but the change benefited everyone. He had more time for outside interests, and he was more engaged and productive at work.

Another category has to do with regular self-reflection. As an example, you might keep a record of your activities, thoughts, and feelings over the course of a month to see how various actions influence your performance and quality of life. Still another category focuses on planning and organizing your time—such as trying out a new technology that coordinates commitments at work with those in the other domains.

Conversations about work and the rest of life tend to emphasize segmentation: How do I shut out the office when I am with my family? How can I eliminate distractions and concentrate purely on work? But, in some cases, it might be better to make boundaries between domains more permeable, not thicker. The very technologies that make it hard for us to maintain healthy boundaries among domains also enable us to blend them in ways—unfathomable even a decade ago—that can render us more productive and more fulfilled. These tools give us choices. The challenge we all face is learning how to use

How Can I Design an Experiment to Improve All Domains of My Life?

Our research has revealed that most successful experiments combine components of nine general categories. Thinking about possibilities in this way will make it easier for you to conceive of the small changes you can make that will mutually benefit your work, your home, your community, and yourself. Most experiments are a hybrid of some combination of these categories.

Tracking and Reflecting

Keeping a record of activities, thoughts, and feelings (and perhaps distributing it to friends, family, and coworkers) to assess progress on personal and professional goals, thereby increasing self-awareness and maintaining priorities.

Examples
- Record visits to the gym along with changes in energy levels
- Track the times of day when you feel most engaged or most lethargic

Planning and Organizing

Taking actions designed to better use time and prepare and plan for the future.

Examples
- Use a PDA for all activities, not just work
- Share your schedule with someone else
- Prepare for the week on Sunday evening

Rejuvenating and Restoring

Attending to body, mind, and spirit so that the tasks of daily living and working are undertaken with renewed power, focus, and commitment.

Examples
- Quit unhealthy physical habits (smoking, drinking)
- Make time for reading a novel
- Engage in activities that improve emotional and spiritual health (yoga, meditation, etc.)

Appreciating and Caring

Having fun with people (typically, by doing things with coworkers outside work), caring for others, and appreciating relationships as a way of bonding at a basic human level to respect the whole person, which increases trust.

Examples
- Join a book group or health club with coworkers
- Help your son complete his homework
- Devote one day a month to community service

Focusing and Concentrating

Being physically present, psychologically present, or both when needed to pay attention to stakeholders who matter most. Sometimes this means saying no to opportunities or obligations. Includes attempts to show more respect to important people encountered in different domains and the need to be accessible to them.

Examples
- Turn off digital communication devices at a set time
- Set aside a specific time to focus on one thing or person
- Review e-mail at preset times during the day

Revealing and Engaging

Sharing more of yourself with others—and listening—so they can better support your values and the steps you want to take toward your leadership vision. By enhancing communication about different aspects of life, you demonstrate respect for the whole person.

Examples
- Have weekly conversations about religion with spouse
- Describe your vision to others
- Mentor a new employee

Time Shifting and "Re-Placing"

Working remotely or during different hours to increase flexibility and thus better fit in community, family, and personal activities while increasing efficiency; questioning traditional assumptions and trying new ways to get things done.

Examples
- Work from home
- Take music lessons during your lunch hour
- Do work during your commute

Delegating and Developing

Reallocating tasks in ways that increase trust, free up time, and develop skills in yourself and others; working smarter by reducing or eliminating low-priority activities.

Examples
- Hire a personal assistant
- Have a subordinate take on some of your responsibilities

Exploring and Venturing

Taking steps toward a new job, career, or other activity that better aligns your work, home, community, and self with your core values and aspirations.

Examples
- Take on new roles at work, such as a cross-functional assignment
- Try a new coaching style
- Join the board of your child's day care center

them wisely, and smart experiments give you an opportunity to increase your skill in doing so. The main point is to identify possibilities that will work well in your unique situation.

All effective experiments require that you question traditional assumptions about how things get done, as the sales director did. It's easier to feel free to do this, and to take innovative action, when you know that your goal is to improve performance in all domains and that you'll be gathering data about the impact of your experiment to determine if indeed it is working—for your key stakeholders and for you.

Whatever type you choose, the most useful experiments feel like something of a stretch: not too easy, not too daunting. It might be something quite mundane for someone else, but that doesn't matter. What's critical is that *you* see it as a moderately difficult challenge.

Choose a few, get started, and adapt. Coming up with possibilities is an exercise in unbounded imagination. But when it comes time to take action, it's not practical to try out more than three experiments at once. Typically, two turn out to be relatively successful and one goes haywire, so you will earn some small wins, and learn something useful about leadership, without biting off more than you can chew. Now the priority is to narrow the list to the three most-promising candidates by reviewing which will:
• Give you the best overall return on your investment
• Be the most costly in regret and missed opportunities if you don't do it
• Allow you to practice the leadership skills you most want to develop
• Be the most fun by involving more of what you want to be doing
• Move you furthest toward your vision of how you want to lead your life

Once you choose and begin to move down the road with your experiment, however, be prepared to adapt to the unforeseen. Don't become too wedded to the details of any one experiment's plan, because you will at some point be surprised and need to adjust. An executive I'll call Lim, for example, chose as one experiment to run the Chicago Marathon. He had been feeling out of shape, which in turn diminished his energy and focus both at work and at home. His wife, Joanne, was pregnant with their first child and initially supported

the plan because she believed that the focus required by the training and the physical outlet it provided would make Lim a better father. The family also had a strong tradition of athleticism, and Joanne herself was an accomplished athlete. Lim was training with his boss and other colleagues, and all agreed that it would be a healthy endeavor that would improve professional communication (as they thought there would be plenty of time to bond during training).

But as her delivery date approached, Joanne became apprehensive, which she expressed to Lim as concern that he might get injured. Her real concern, though, was that he was spending so much time on an activity that might drain his energy at a point when the family needed him most. One adjustment that Lim made to reassure Joanne of his commitment to their family was to initiate another experiment in which he took the steps needed to allow him to work at home on Thursday afternoons. He had to set up some new technologies and agree to send a monthly memo to his boss summarizing what he was accomplishing on those afternoons. He also bought a baby sling, which would allow him to keep his new son with him while at home.

In the end, not only were Joanne and their baby on hand to cheer Lim on while he ran the marathon, but she ended up joining him for the second half of the race to give him a boost when she saw his energy flagging. His business unit's numbers improved during the period when he was training and working at home. So did the unit's morale—people began to see the company as more flexible, and they were encouraged to be more creative in how they got their own work done—and word got around. Executives throughout the firm began to come up with their own ideas for ways to pay more attention to other sides of their employees' lives and so build a stronger sense of community at work.

The investment in a well-designed experiment almost always pays off because you learn how to lead in new and creative ways in all parts of your life. And if your experiments turn out well—as they usually, but not always, do—it will benefit everyone: you, your business, your family, and your community.

Measuring Progress
The only way to fail with an experiment is to

Typically, two experiments turn out to be relatively successful and one goes haywire.

fail to learn from it, and this makes useful metrics essential. No doubt it's better to achieve the results you are after than to fall short, but hitting targets does not in itself advance you toward becoming the leader you want to be. Failed experiments give you, and those around you, information that helps create better ones in the future.

The exhibit "How Do I Know If My Experiment Is Working?" shows how Kenneth Chen measured his progress. He used this simple chart to spell out the intended benefits of his experiment in each of the four domains and how he would assess whether he had realized these benefits. To set up your own scorecard, use a separate sheet for each experiment; at the top of the page, write a brief description of it. Then record your goals for each domain in the first column. In the middle column, describe your results metrics: how you will measure whether the goals for each domain have been achieved. In the third column, describe your action metrics—the plan for the steps you will take to implement your experiment. As you begin to implement your plan, you may find that your initial indicators are too broad or too vague, so refine your scorecard as you go along to make it more useful for you. The main point is to have practical ways of measuring your outcomes and your progress toward them, and the approach you take only needs to work for you and your stakeholders.

How Do I Know If My Experiment Is Working?

Using this tool, an executive I'll call Kenneth Chen systematically set out in detail his various goals, the metrics he would use to measure his progress, and the steps he would take in conducting an experiment that would further those goals—joining the board of a nonprofit organization. Kenneth's work sheet is merely an example: Every person's experiments, goals, and metrics are unique.

A Sample Scorecard:

	EXPERIMENT'S GOALS	HOW I WILL MEASURE SUCCESS	IMPLEMENTATION STEPS
Work	▶ To fulfill the expectation that executives will give back to the local community ▶ To establish networks with other officers in my company and other professionals in the area ▶ To learn leadership skills from other board members and from the organization I join	▶ Collect business cards from everyone I meet on the board and during board meetings, and keep track of the number of professionals I meet ▶ After each meeting, regularly record the leadership skills of those I would like to emulate	❑ Meet with my manager, who has sat on many boards and can provide support and advice ❑ Meet with the director of my company's foundation to determine my real interests and to help assess what relationship our firm has with various community organizations ❑ Discuss my course of action with my fiancée and see whether joining a board interests her ❑ Sign up to attend the December 15 overview session of the Business on Board program ❑ Assess different opportunities within the community and then reach out to organizations I'm interested in ❑ Apply for membership to a community board
Home	▶ To join a board that can involve my fiancée, Celine ▶ To have something to discuss with my sister (a special-education instructor)	▶ See whether Celine gets involved in the board ▶ Record the number of conversations my sister and I have about community service for the next three months and see whether they have brought us closer	
Community	▶ To provide my leadership skills to a nonprofit organization ▶ To get more involved in giving back to the community	▶ Record what I learn about each nonprofit organization I research ▶ Record the number of times I attend board meetings	
Self	▶ To feel good about contributing to others' welfare ▶ To see others grow as a result of my efforts ▶ To become more compassionate	▶ Assess how I feel about myself in a daily journal ▶ Assess the effect I have on others in terms of potential number of people affected ▶ Ask for feedback from others about whether I've become more compassionate	

Visit richerlife.tools.hbr.org for further work sheets and for blank versions to download. For a more comprehensive offering of online tools, videos, and blogs, go to www.totalleadership.org.

Workshop participants have used all kinds of metrics: cost savings from reduced travel, number of e-mail misunderstandings averted, degree of satisfaction with family time, hours spent volunteering at a teen center, and so on. Metrics may be objective or subjective, qualitative or quantitative, reported by you or by others, and frequently or intermittently observed. When it comes to frequency, for instance, it helps to consider how long you'll be able to remember what you did. For example, if you were to go on a diet to get healthier, increase energy, and enhance key relationships, food intake would be an important metric. But would you be able to remember what you ate two days ago?

Small Wins for Big Change

Experiments shouldn't be massive, all-encompassing shifts in the way you live. Highly ambitious designs usually fail because they're too much to handle. The best experiments let you try something new while minimizing the inevitable risks associated with change. When the stakes are smaller, it's easier to overcome the fear of failure that inhibits innovation. You start to see results, and others take note, which both inspires you to go further and builds support from your key stakeholders.

Another benefit of the small-wins approach to experiments is that it opens doors that would otherwise be closed. You can say to people invested in the decision, "Let's just try this. If it doesn't work, we'll go back to the old way or try something different." By framing an experiment as a trial, you reduce resistance because people are more likely to try something new if they know it's not permanent and if they have control over deciding whether the experiment is working according to *their* performance expectations.

But "small" is a relative term—what might look like a small step for you could seem like a giant leap to me, and vice versa. So don't get hung up on the word. What's more, this isn't about the scope or importance of the changes you eventually make. Large-scale change is grounded in small steps toward a big idea. So while the steps in an experiment might be small, the goals are not. Ismail, a successful 50-year-old entrepreneur and CEO of an engineering services company, described the goal for his first experiment this way: "Restructure

my company and my role in it." There's nothing small about that. He felt he was missing a sense of purpose.

Ismail designed practical steps that would allow him to move toward his large goal over time. His first experiments were small and achievable. He introduced a new method that both his colleagues and his wife could use to communicate with him. He began to hold sacrosanct time for his family and his church. As he looked for ways to free up more time, he initiated delegation experiments that had the effect of flattening his organization's structure. These small wins crossed over several domains, and eventually he did indeed transform his company and his own role in it. When I spoke with him 18 months after he'd started, he acknowledged that he'd had a hard time coping with the loss of control over tactical business matters, but he described his experiments as "a testament to the idea of winning the small battles and letting the war be won as a result." He and his leadership team both felt more confident about the firm's new organizational structure.

• • •

People try the Total Leadership program for a variety of reasons. Some feel unfulfilled because they're not doing what they love. Some don't feel genuine because they're not acting according to their values. Others feel disconnected, isolated from people who matter to them. They crave stronger relationships, built on trust, and yearn for enriched social networks. Still others are just in a rut. They want to tap into their creative energy but don't know how (and sometimes lack the courage) to do so. They feel out of control and unable to fit in all that's important to them.

My hunch is that there are more four-way wins available to you than you'd think. They are there for the taking. You have to know how to look for them and then find the support and zeal to pursue them. By providing a blueprint for how you can be real, be whole, and be innovative as a leader in all parts of your life, this program helps you perform better according to the standards of the most important people in your life; feel better in all the domains of your life; and foster greater harmony among the domains by increasing the resources available to you to fit all the parts of your life together. No matter what your career stage or current position, you

You can say to people: "Let's just try this. If it doesn't work, we'll go back to the old way or try something different."

can be a better leader and have a richer life—
if you are ready and willing to rise to the
challenge.

Reprint R0804H
To order, see the next page
or call 800-988-0886 or 617-783-7500
or go to www.hbr.org

Be a Better Leader, Have a Richer Life

Further Reading

BOOK

Total Leadership: Be a Better Leader, Have a Richer Life
by Stewart D. Friedman
Harvard Business Press
June 2008
Product no. 3285

This book, on which the article is based, offers additional ideas on how to perform well as a leader, not by trading off one life domain for another, but by finding mutual value among all four—work, home, community, and self. The author shows you how to achieve these "four-way wins" as a leader who can: **Be real**—act with *authenticity* by clarifying what's important; **Be whole**—act with *integrity* by respecting the whole person; and **Be innovative**—act with *creativity* by experimenting to find new solutions. The book includes more than 30 hands-on tools to help you produce stronger business results, find clearer purpose in what you do, feel more connected to the people who matter most, and generate sustainable change.

ARTICLES

Work and Life: The End of the Zero-Sum Game
by Stewart D. Friedman, Perry Christensen, and Jessica DeGroot
Harvard Business Review
July 2000
Product no. 4452

Not only do successful leaders pay attention to all dimensions of their lives—they encourage their employees to do the same. Leaders who treat employees' work and personal lives as complementary, not competing, priorities discover that employees respond with greater effort and loyalty. To create a work environment that supports all domains of employees' lives: 1) **Clarify what's important.** Be explicit about your unit's priorities and your expectations for employees' performance, but give employees great autonomy over how to achieve the goals you've laid out. At the same time, encourage employees to identify their concerns and goals outside the office. 2) **Take time to learn about employees' personal situations.** Not only does this build trust, it also creates opportunities to learn about other talents that employees could bring to your business. 3) **Continually experiment with how work gets done.** Streamlining work processes can improve performance and give employees more time to pursue personal goals.

Success That Lasts
by Laura Nash and Howard Stevenson
Harvard Business Review
April 2004
Product no. 659X

These authors provide another process for determining what matters most to you, a step you take before designing experiments for change. First, imagine life satisfaction as consisting of four categories: happiness, achievement, significance (positively affecting those you care about), and legacy (helping others find future success). Second, assess the various categories of satisfaction you've already experienced. Third, notice patterns: Are some categories meager? Others too full? Are the patterns in line with your goals? Fourth, identify which categories need attention and which show "just enough" success so that you can focus your efforts on a different category.

Harvard Business Review 🛡

To Order

For *Harvard Business Review* reprints and subscriptions, call 800-988-0886 or 617-783-7500. Go to www.hbr.org

For customized and quantity orders of *Harvard Business Review* article reprints, call 617-783-7626, or e-mail customizations@hbsp.harvard.edu

Harvard Business Review

www.hbr.org

BEST OF HBR 1999

Success in the knowledge economy comes to those who know themselves—their strengths, their values, and how they best perform.

Managing Oneself

by Peter F. Drucker

Included with this full-text *Harvard Business Review* article:

Reprint R0501K

Managing Oneself

The Idea in Brief

We live in an age of unprecedented opportunity: If you've got ambition, drive, and smarts, you can rise to the top of your chosen profession—regardless of where you started out. But with opportunity comes responsibility. Companies today aren't managing their knowledge workers' careers. Rather, we must each be our own chief executive officer.

Simply put, it's up to you to carve out your place in the work world and know when to change course. And it's up to you to keep yourself engaged and productive during a work life that may span some 50 years.

To do all of these things well, you'll need to cultivate a deep understanding of yourself. What are your most valuable strengths and most dangerous weaknesses? Equally important, how do you learn and work with others? What are your most deeply held values? And in what type of work environment can you make the greatest contribution?

The implication is clear: Only when you operate from a combination of your strengths and self-knowledge can you achieve true—and lasting—excellence.

The Idea in Practice

To build a life of excellence, begin by asking yourself these questions:

"What are my strengths?"

To accurately identify your strengths, use **feedback analysis**. Every time you make a key decision, write down the outcome you expect. Several months later, compare the actual results with your expected results. Look for patterns in what you're seeing: What results are you skilled at generating? What abilities do you need to enhance in order to get the results you want? What unproductive habits are preventing you from creating the outcomes you desire? In identifying opportunities for improvement, don't waste time cultivating skill areas where you have little competence. Instead, concentrate on—and build on—your strengths

"How do I work?"

In what ways do you work best? Do you process information most effectively by reading it, or by hearing others discuss it? Do you accomplish the most by working with other people, or by working alone? Do you perform best while making decisions, or while advising others on key matters? Are you in top form when things get stressful, or do you function optimally in a highly predictable environment?

"What are my values?"

What are your ethics? What do you see as your most important responsibilities for living a worthy, ethical life? Do your organization's ethics resonate with your own values? If not, your career will likely be marked by frustration and poor performance.

"Where do I belong?"

Consider your strengths, preferred work style, and values. Based on these qualities, in what kind of work environment would you fit in best? Find the perfect fit, and you'll transform yourself from a merely acceptable employee into a star performer.

"What can I contribute?"

In earlier eras, companies told businesspeople what their contribution should be. Today, you have choices. To decide how you can best enhance your organization's performance, first ask what the situation requires. Based on your strengths, work style, and values, how might you make the greatest contribution to your organization's efforts?

Success in the knowledge economy comes to those who know themselves—their strengths, their values, and how they best perform.

Managing Oneself

by Peter F. Drucker

We live in an age of unprecedented opportunity: If you've got ambition and smarts, you can rise to the top of your chosen profession, regardless of where you started out.

But with opportunity comes responsibility. Companies today aren't managing their employees' careers; knowledge workers must, effectively, be their own chief executive officers. It's up to you to carve out your place, to know when to change course, and to keep yourself engaged and productive during a work life that may span some 50 years. To do those things well, you'll need to cultivate a deep understanding of yourself—not only what your strengths and weaknesses are but also how you learn, how you work with others, what your values are, and where you can make the greatest contribution. Because only when you operate from strengths can you achieve true excellence.

History's great achievers—a Napoléon, a da Vinci, a Mozart—have always managed themselves. That, in large measure, is what makes them great achievers. But they are rare excep-

tions, so unusual both in their talents and their accomplishments as to be considered outside the boundaries of ordinary human existence. Now, most of us, even those of us with modest endowments, will have to learn to manage ourselves. We will have to learn to develop ourselves. We will have to place ourselves where we can make the greatest contribution. And we will have to stay mentally alert and engaged during a 50-year working life, which means knowing how and when to change the work we do.

What Are My Strengths?

Most people think they know what they are good at. They are usually wrong. More often, people know what they are not good at—and even then more people are wrong than right. And yet, a person can perform only from strength. One cannot build performance on weaknesses, let alone on something one cannot do at all.

Throughout history, people had little need to know their strengths. A person was born into a position and a line of work: The peasant's son would also be a peasant; the artisan's daughter, an artisan's wife; and so on. But now people have choices. We need to know our strengths in order to know where we belong.

The only way to discover your strengths is through feedback analysis. Whenever you make a key decision or take a key action, write down what you expect will happen. Nine or 12 months later, compare the actual results with your expectations. I have been practicing this method for 15 to 20 years now, and every time I do it, I am surprised. The feedback analysis showed me, for instance—and to my great surprise—that I have an intuitive understanding of technical people, whether they are engineers or accountants or market researchers. It also showed me that I don't really resonate with generalists.

Feedback analysis is by no means new. It was invented sometime in the fourteenth century by an otherwise totally obscure German theologian and picked up quite independently, some 150 years later, by John Calvin and Ignatius of Loyola, each of whom incorporated it into the practice of his followers. In fact, the steadfast focus on performance and results that this habit produces explains why the institutions these two men founded, the Calvinist church and the Jesuit order, came to dominate Europe within 30 years.

Practiced consistently, this simple method will show you within a fairly short period of time, maybe two or three years, where your strengths lie—and this is the most important thing to know. The method will show you what you are doing or failing to do that deprives you of the full benefits of your strengths. It will show you where you are not particularly competent. And finally, it will show you where you have no strengths and cannot perform.

Several implications for action follow from feedback analysis. First and foremost, concentrate on your strengths. Put yourself where your strengths can produce results.

Second, work on improving your strengths. Analysis will rapidly show where you need to improve skills or acquire new ones. It will also show the gaps in your knowledge—and those can usually be filled. Mathematicians are born, but everyone can learn trigonometry.

Third, discover where your intellectual arro-

gance is causing disabling ignorance and overcome it. Far too many people—especially people with great expertise in one area—are contemptuous of knowledge in other areas or believe that being bright is a substitute for knowledge. First-rate engineers, for instance, tend to take pride in not knowing anything about people. Human beings, they believe, are much too disorderly for the good engineering mind. Human resources professionals, by contrast, often pride themselves on their ignorance of elementary accounting or of quantitative methods altogether. But taking pride in such ignorance is self-defeating. Go to work on acquiring the skills and knowledge you need to fully realize your strengths.

It is equally essential to remedy your bad habits—the things you do or fail to do that inhibit your effectiveness and performance. Such habits will quickly show up in the feedback. For example, a planner may find that his beautiful plans fail because he does not follow through on them. Like so many brilliant people, he believes that ideas move mountains. But bulldozers move mountains; ideas show where the bulldozers should go to work. This planner will have to learn that the work does not stop when the plan is completed. He must find people to carry out the plan and explain it to them. He must adapt and change it as he puts it into action. And finally, he must decide when to stop pushing the plan.

At the same time, feedback will also reveal when the problem is a lack of manners. Manners are the lubricating oil of an organization. It is a law of nature that two moving bodies in contact with each other create friction. This is as true for human beings as it is for inanimate objects. Manners—simple things like saying "please" and "thank you" and knowing a person's name or asking after her family—enable two people to work together whether they like each other or not. Bright people, especially bright young people, often do not understand this. If analysis shows that someone's brilliant work fails again and again as soon as cooperation from others is required, it probably indicates a lack of courtesy—that is, a lack of manners.

Comparing your expectations with your results also indicates what not to do. We all have a vast number of areas in which we have no talent or skill and little chance of becoming even mediocre. In those areas a person—

Peter F. Drucker is the Marie Rankin Clarke Professor of Social Science and Management (Emeritus) at Claremont Graduate University in Claremont, California. This article is an excerpt from his book *Management Challenges for the 21st Century* (HarperCollins, 1999).

and especially a knowledge worker—should not take on work, jobs, and assignments. One should waste as little effort as possible on improving areas of low competence. It takes far more energy and work to improve from incompetence to mediocrity than it takes to improve from first-rate performance to excellence. And yet most people—especially most teachers and most organizations—concentrate on making incompetent performers into mediocre ones. Energy, resources, and time should go instead to making a competent person into a star performer.

How Do I Perform?

Amazingly few people know how they get things done. Indeed, most of us do not even know that different people work and perform differently. Too many people work in ways that are not their ways, and that almost guarantees nonperformance. For knowledge workers, How do I perform? may be an even more important question than What are my strengths?

Like one's strengths, how one performs is unique. It is a matter of personality. Whether personality be a matter of nature or nurture, it surely is formed long before a person goes to work. And *how* a person performs is a given, just as *what* a person is good at or not good at is a given. A person's way of performing can be slightly modified, but it is unlikely to be completely changed—and certainly not easily. Just as people achieve results by doing what they are good at, they also achieve results by working in ways that they best perform. A few common personality traits usually determine how a person performs.

Am I a reader or a listener? The first thing to know is whether you are a reader or a listener. Far too few people even know that there are readers and listeners and that people are rarely both. Even fewer know which of the two they themselves are. But some examples will show how damaging such ignorance can be.

When Dwight Eisenhower was Supreme Commander of the Allied forces in Europe, he was the darling of the press. His press conferences were famous for their style—General Eisenhower showed total command of whatever question he was asked, and he was able to describe a situation and explain a policy in two or three beautifully polished and elegant sentences. Ten years later, the same journalists who had been his admirers held President Eisenhower in open contempt. He never addressed the questions, they complained, but rambled on endlessly about something else. And they constantly ridiculed him for butchering the King's English in incoherent and ungrammatical answers.

Eisenhower apparently did not know that he was a reader, not a listener. When he was Supreme Commander in Europe, his aides made sure that every question from the press was presented in writing at least half an hour before a conference was to begin. And then Eisenhower was in total command. When he became president, he succeeded two listeners, Franklin D. Roosevelt and Harry Truman. Both men knew themselves to be listeners and both enjoyed free-for-all press conferences. Eisenhower may have felt that he had to do what his two predecessors had done. As a result, he never even heard the questions journalists asked. And Eisenhower is not even an extreme case of a nonlistener.

A few years later, Lyndon Johnson destroyed his presidency, in large measure, by not knowing that he was a listener. His predecessor, John Kennedy, was a reader who had assembled a brilliant group of writers as his assistants, making sure that they wrote to him before discussing their memos in person. Johnson kept these people on his staff—and they kept on writing. He never, apparently, understood one word of what they wrote. Yet as a senator, Johnson had been superb; for parliamentarians have to be, above all, listeners.

Few listeners can be made, or can make themselves, into competent readers—and vice versa. The listener who tries to be a reader will, therefore, suffer the fate of Lyndon Johnson, whereas the reader who tries to be a listener will suffer the fate of Dwight Eisenhower. They will not perform or achieve.

How do I learn? The second thing to know about how one performs is to know how one learns. Many first-class writers—Winston Churchill is but one example—do poorly in school. They tend to remember their schooling as pure torture. Yet few of their classmates remember it the same way. They may not have enjoyed the school very much, but the worst they suffered was boredom. The explanation is that writers do not, as a rule, learn by listening and reading. They learn by writing. Because schools do not allow them to learn this way,

It takes far more energy to improve from incompetence to mediocrity than to improve from first-rate performance to excellence.

they get poor grades.

Schools everywhere are organized on the assumption that there is only one right way to learn and that it is the same way for everybody. But to be forced to learn the way a school teaches is sheer hell for students who learn differently. Indeed, there are probably half a dozen different ways to learn.

There are people, like Churchill, who learn by writing. Some people learn by taking copious notes. Beethoven, for example, left behind an enormous number of sketchbooks, yet he said he never actually looked at them when he composed. Asked why he kept them, he is reported to have replied, "If I don't write it down immediately, I forget it right away. If I put it into a sketchbook, I never forget it and I never have to look it up again." Some people learn by doing. Others learn by hearing themselves talk.

A chief executive I know who converted a small and mediocre family business into the leading company in its industry was one of those people who learn by talking. He was in the habit of calling his entire senior staff into his office once a week and then talking at them for two or three hours. He would raise policy issues and argue three different positions on each one. He rarely asked his associates for comments or questions; he simply needed an audience to hear himself talk. That's how he learned. And although he is a fairly extreme case, learning through talking is by no means an unusual method. Successful trial lawyers learn the same way, as do many medical diagnosticians (and so do I).

Of all the important pieces of self-knowledge, understanding how you learn is the easiest to acquire. When I ask people, "How do you learn?" most of them know the answer. But when I ask, "Do you act on this knowledge?" few answer yes. And yet, acting on this knowledge is the key to performance; or rather, *not* acting on this knowledge condemns one to nonperformance.

Am I a reader or a listener? and How do I learn? are the first questions to ask. But they are by no means the only ones. To manage yourself effectively, you also have to ask, Do I work well with people, or am I a loner? And if you do work well with people, you then must ask, In what relationship?

Some people work best as subordinates. General George Patton, the great American military hero of World War II, is a prime example. Patton

Do not try to change yourself—you are unlikely to succeed. Work to improve the way you perform.

was America's top troop commander. Yet when he was proposed for an independent command, General George Marshall, the U.S. chief of staff—and probably the most successful picker of men in U.S. history—said, "Patton is the best subordinate the American army has ever produced, but he would be the worst commander."

Some people work best as team members. Others work best alone. Some are exceptionally talented as coaches and mentors; others are simply incompetent as mentors.

Another crucial question is, Do I produce results as a decision maker or as an adviser? A great many people perform best as advisers but cannot take the burden and pressure of making the decision. A good many other people, by contrast, need an adviser to force themselves to think; then they can make decisions and act on them with speed, self-confidence, and courage.

This is a reason, by the way, that the number two person in an organization often fails when promoted to the number one position. The top spot requires a decision maker. Strong decision makers often put somebody they trust into the number two spot as their adviser—and in that position the person is outstanding. But in the number one spot, the same person fails. He or she knows what the decision should be but cannot accept the responsibility of actually making it.

Other important questions to ask include, Do I perform well under stress, or do I need a highly structured and predictable environment? Do I work best in a big organization or a small one? Few people work well in all kinds of environments. Again and again, I have seen people who were very successful in large organizations flounder miserably when they moved into smaller ones. And the reverse is equally true.

The conclusion bears repeating: Do not try to change yourself—you are unlikely to succeed. But work hard to improve the way you perform. And try not to take on work you cannot perform or will only perform poorly.

What Are My Values?

To be able to manage yourself, you finally have to ask, What are my values? This is not a question of ethics. With respect to ethics, the rules are the same for everybody, and the test is a simple one. I call it the "mirror test."

In the early years of this century, the most

highly respected diplomat of all the great powers was the German ambassador in London. He was clearly destined for great things—to become his country's foreign minister, at least, if not its federal chancellor. Yet in 1906 he abruptly resigned rather than preside over a dinner given by the diplomatic corps for Edward VII. The king was a notorious womanizer and made it clear what kind of dinner he wanted. The ambassador is reported to have said, "I refuse to see a pimp in the mirror in the morning when I shave."

That is the mirror test. Ethics requires that you ask yourself, What kind of person do I want to see in the mirror in the morning? What is ethical behavior in one kind of organization or situation is ethical behavior in another. But ethics is only part of a value system—especially of an organization's value system.

To work in an organization whose value system is unacceptable or incompatible with one's own condemns a person both to frustration and to nonperformance.

Consider the experience of a highly successful human resources executive whose company was acquired by a bigger organization. After the acquisition, she was promoted to do the kind of work she did best, which included selecting people for important positions. The executive deeply believed that a company should hire people for such positions from the outside only after exhausting all the inside possibilities. But her new company believed in first looking outside "to bring in fresh blood." There is something to be said for both approaches—in my experience, the proper one is to do some of both. They are, however, fundamentally incompatible—not as policies but as values. They bespeak different views of the relationship between organizations and people; different views of the responsibility of an organization to its people and their development; and different views of a person's most important contribution to an enterprise. After several years of frustration, the executive quit—at considerable financial loss. Her values and the values of the organization simply were not compatible.

Similarly, whether a pharmaceutical company tries to obtain results by making constant, small improvements or by achieving occasional, highly expensive, and risky "breakthroughs" is not primarily an economic question. The results of either strategy may be pretty much the same. At bottom, there is a conflict between a value system that sees the company's contribution in terms of helping physicians do better what they already do and a value system that is oriented toward making scientific discoveries.

Whether a business should be run for short-term results or with a focus on the long term is likewise a question of values. Financial analysts believe that businesses can be run for both simultaneously. Successful businesspeople know better. To be sure, every company has to produce short-term results. But in any conflict between short-term results and long-term growth, each company will determine its own priority. This is not primarily a disagreement about economics. It is fundamentally a value conflict regarding the function of a business and the responsibility of management.

Value conflicts are not limited to business organizations. One of the fastest-growing pastoral churches in the United States measures success by the number of new parishioners. Its leadership believes that what matters is how many newcomers join the congregation. The Good Lord will then minister to their spiritual needs or at least to the needs of a sufficient percentage. Another pastoral, evangelical church believes that what matters is people's spiritual growth. The church eases out newcomers who join but do not enter into its spiritual life.

Again, this is not a matter of numbers. At first glance, it appears that the second church grows more slowly. But it retains a far larger proportion of newcomers than the first one does. Its growth, in other words, is more solid. This is also not a theological problem, or only secondarily so. It is a problem about values. In a public debate, one pastor argued, "Unless you first come to church, you will never find the gate to the Kingdom of Heaven."

"No," answered the other. "Until you first look for the gate to the Kingdom of Heaven, you don't belong in church."

Organizations, like people, have values. To be effective in an organization, a person's values must be compatible with the organization's values. They do not need to be the same, but they must be close enough to coexist. Otherwise, the person will not only be frustrated but also will not produce results.

A person's strengths and the way that person performs rarely conflict; the two are complementary. But there is sometimes a conflict between a person's values and his or her strengths. What one does well—even very well and successfully—may not fit with one's value system. In that case, the work may not appear to be worth devoting one's life to (or even a substantial portion thereof).

If I may, allow me to interject a personal note. Many years ago, I too had to decide between my values and what I was doing successfully. I was doing very well as a young investment banker in London in the mid-1930s, and the work clearly fit my strengths. Yet I did not see myself making a contribution as an asset manager. People, I realized, were what I valued, and I saw no point in being the richest man in the cemetery. I had no money and no other job prospects. Despite the continuing Depression, I quit—and it was the right thing to do. Values, in other words, are and should be the ultimate test.

Where Do I Belong?

A small number of people know very early where they belong. Mathematicians, musicians, and cooks, for instance, are usually mathematicians, musicians, and cooks by the time they are four or five years old. Physicians usually decide on their careers in their teens, if not earlier. But most people, especially highly gifted people, do not really know where they belong until they are well past their mid-twenties. By that time, however, they should know the answers to the three questions: What are my strengths? How do I perform? and, What are my values? And then they can and should decide where they belong.

Or rather, they should be able to decide where they do *not* belong. The person who has learned that he or she does not perform well in a big organization should have learned to say no to a position in one. The person who has learned that he or she is not a decision maker should have learned to say no to a decision-making assignment. A General Patton (who probably never learned this himself) should have learned to say no to an independent command.

Equally important, knowing the answer to these questions enables a person to say to an opportunity, an offer, or an assignment, "Yes, I will do that. But this is the way I should be doing it. This is the way it should be structured. This is the way the relationships should be. These are the kind of results you should expect from me, and in this time frame, because this is who I am."

Successful careers are not planned. They develop when people are prepared for opportunities because they know their strengths, their method of work, and their values. Knowing where one belongs can transform an ordinary person—hardworking and competent but otherwise mediocre—into an outstanding performer.

What Should I Contribute?

Throughout history, the great majority of people never had to ask the question, What should I contribute? They were told what to contribute, and their tasks were dictated either by the work itself—as it was for the peasant or artisan—or by a master or a mistress—as it was for domestic servants. And until very recently, it was taken for granted that most people were subordinates who did as they were told. Even in the 1950s and 1960s, the new knowledge workers (the so-called organization men) looked to their company's personnel department to plan their careers.

Then in the late 1960s, no one wanted to be told what to do any longer. Young men and women began to ask, What do *I* want to do? And what they heard was that the way to contribute was to "do your own thing." But this solution was as wrong as the organization men's had been. Very few of the people who believed that doing one's own thing would lead to contribution, self-fulfillment, and success achieved any of the three.

But still, there is no return to the old answer of doing what you are told or assigned to do. Knowledge workers in particular have to learn to ask a question that has not been asked before: What *should* my contribution be? To answer it, they must address three distinct elements: What does the situation require? Given my strengths, my way of performing, and my values, how can I make the greatest contribution to what needs to be done? And finally, What results have to be achieved to make a difference?

Consider the experience of a newly appointed hospital administrator. The hospital was big and prestigious, but it had been coasting on its reputation for 30 years. The

What one does well— even very well and successfully—may not fit with one's value system.

new administrator decided that his contribution should be to establish a standard of excellence in one important area within two years. He chose to focus on the emergency room, which was big, visible, and sloppy. He decided that every patient who came into the ER had to be seen by a qualified nurse within 60 seconds. Within 12 months, the hospital's emergency room had become a model for all hospitals in the United States, and within another two years, the whole hospital had been transformed.

As this example suggests, it is rarely possible—or even particularly fruitful—to look too far ahead. A plan can usually cover no more than 18 months and still be reasonably clear and specific. So the question in most cases should be, Where and how can I achieve results that will make a difference within the next year and a half? The answer must balance several things. First, the results should be hard to achieve—they should require "stretching," to use the current buzzword. But also, they should be within reach. To aim at results that cannot be achieved—or that can be only under the most unlikely circumstances—is not being ambitious; it is being foolish. Second, the results should be meaningful. They should make a difference. Finally, results should be visible and, if at all possible, measurable. From this will come a course of action: what to do, where and how to start, and what goals and deadlines to set.

Responsibility for Relationships

Very few people work by themselves and achieve results by themselves—a few great artists, a few great scientists, a few great athletes. Most people work with others and are effective with other people. That is true whether they are members of an organization or independently employed. Managing yourself requires taking responsibility for relationships. This has two parts.

The first is to accept the fact that other people are as much individuals as you yourself are. They perversely insist on behaving like human beings. This means that they too have their strengths; they too have their ways of getting things done; they too have their values. To be effective, therefore, you have to know the strengths, the performance modes, and the values of your coworkers.

That sounds obvious, but few people pay at-

tention to it. Typical is the person who was trained to write reports in his or her first assignment because that boss was a reader. Even if the next boss is a listener, the person goes on writing reports that, invariably, produce no results. Invariably the boss will think the employee is stupid, incompetent, and lazy, and he or she will fail. But that could have been avoided if the employee had only looked at the new boss and analyzed how *this* boss performs.

Bosses are neither a title on the organization chart nor a "function." They are individuals and are entitled to do their work in the way they do it best. It is incumbent on the people who work with them to observe them, to find out how they work, and to adapt themselves to what makes their bosses most effective. This, in fact, is the secret of "managing" the boss.

The same holds true for all your coworkers. Each works his or her way, not your way. And each is entitled to work in his or her way. What matters is whether they perform and what their values are. As for how they perform—each is likely to do it differently. The first secret of effectiveness is to understand the people you work with and depend on so that you can make use of their strengths, their ways of working, and their values. Working relationships are as much based on the people as they are on the work.

The second part of relationship responsibility is taking responsibility for communication. Whenever I, or any other consultant, start to work with an organization, the first thing I hear about are all the personality conflicts. Most of these arise from the fact that people do not know what other people are doing and how they do their work, or what contribution the other people are concentrating on and what results they expect. And the reason they do not know is that they have not asked and therefore have not been told.

This failure to ask reflects human stupidity less than it reflects human history. Until recently, it was unnecessary to tell any of these things to anybody. In the medieval city, everyone in a district plied the same trade. In the countryside, everyone in a valley planted the same crop as soon as the frost was out of the ground. Even those few people who did things that were not "common" worked alone, so they did not have to tell anyone what they were doing.

Today the great majority of people work

The first secret of effectiveness is to understand the people you work with so that you can make use of their strengths.

with others who have different tasks and responsibilities. The marketing vice president may have come out of sales and know everything about sales, but she knows nothing about the things she has never done—pricing, advertising, packaging, and the like. So the people who do these things must make sure that the marketing vice president understands what they are trying to do, why they are trying to do it, how they are going to do it, and what results to expect.

If the marketing vice president does not understand what these high-grade knowledge specialists are doing, it is primarily their fault, not hers. They have not educated her. Conversely, it is the marketing vice president's responsibility to make sure that all of her co-workers understand how she looks at marketing: what her goals are, how she works, and what she expects of herself and of each one of them.

Even people who understand the importance of taking responsibility for relationships often do not communicate sufficiently with their associates. They are afraid of being thought presumptuous or inquisitive or stupid. They are wrong. Whenever someone goes to his or her associates and says, "This is what I am good at. This is how I work. These are my values. This is the contribution I plan to concentrate on and the results I should be expected to deliver," the response is always, "This is most helpful. But why didn't you tell me earlier?"

And one gets the same reaction—without exception, in my experience—if one continues by asking, "And what do I need to know about your strengths, how you perform, your values, and your proposed contribution?" In fact, knowledge workers should request this of everyone with whom they work, whether as subordinate, superior, colleague, or team member. And again, whenever this is done, the reaction is always, "Thanks for asking me. But why didn't you ask me earlier?"

Organizations are no longer built on force but on trust. The existence of trust between people does not necessarily mean that they like one another. It means that they understand one another. Taking responsibility for relationships is therefore an absolute necessity. It is a duty. Whether one is a member of the organization, a consultant to it, a supplier, or a distributor, one owes that responsibility to all one's coworkers: those whose work one depends on as well as those who depend on one's own work.

The Second Half of Your Life

When work for most people meant manual labor, there was no need to worry about the second half of your life. You simply kept on doing what you had always done. And if you were lucky enough to survive 40 years of hard work in the mill or on the railroad, you were quite happy to spend the rest of your life doing nothing. Today, however, most work is knowledge work, and knowledge workers are not "finished" after 40 years on the job, they are merely bored.

We hear a great deal of talk about the midlife crisis of the executive. It is mostly boredom. At 45, most executives have reached the peak of their business careers, and they know it. After 20 years of doing very much the same kind of work, they are very good at their jobs. But they are not learning or contributing or deriving challenge and satisfaction from the job. And yet they are still likely to face another 20 if not 25 years of work. That is why managing oneself increasingly leads one to begin a second career.

There are three ways to develop a second career. The first is actually to start one. Often this takes nothing more than moving from one kind of organization to another: the divisional controller in a large corporation, for instance, becomes the controller of a medium-sized hospital. But there are also growing numbers of people who move into different lines of work altogether: the business executive or government official who enters the ministry at 45, for instance; or the midlevel manager who leaves corporate life after 20 years to attend law school and become a small-town attorney.

We will see many more second careers undertaken by people who have achieved modest success in their first jobs. Such people have substantial skills, and they know how to work. They need a community—the house is empty with the children gone—and they need income as well. But above all, they need challenge.

The second way to prepare for the second half of your life is to develop a parallel career. Many people who are very successful in their first careers stay in the work they have been doing, either on a full-time or part-time or consulting basis. But in addition, they create a parallel job, usually in a nonprofit organization, that takes another ten hours of work a week. They might take over the administration of their church, for instance, or the presidency of the local Girl Scouts council. They might run the battered women's shelter, work as a children's librarian for the local public library, sit on the school board, and so on.

Finally, there are the social entrepreneurs. These are usually people who have been very successful in their first careers. They love their work, but it no longer challenges them. In many cases they keep on doing what they have been doing all along but spend less and less of their time on it. They also start another activity, usually a nonprofit. My friend Bob Buford, for example, built a very successful television company that he still runs. But he has also founded and built a successful nonprofit organization that works with Protestant churches, and he is building another to teach social entrepreneurs how to manage their own nonprofit ventures while still running their original businesses.

People who manage the second half of their lives may always be a minority. The majority may "retire on the job" and count the years until their actual retirement. But it is this minority, the men and women who see a long working-life expectancy as an opportunity both for themselves and for society, who will become leaders and models.

There is one prerequisite for managing the second half of your life: You must begin long before you enter it. When it first became clear 30 years ago that working-life expectancies were lengthening very fast, many observers (including myself) believed that retired people would increasingly become volunteers for nonprofit institutions. That has not happened. If one does not begin to volunteer before one is 40 or so, one will not volunteer once past 60.

Similarly, all the social entrepreneurs I know began to work in their chosen second enterprise long before they reached their peak in their original business. Consider the example of a successful lawyer, the legal counsel to a large corporation, who has started a venture to establish model schools in his state. He began to do volunteer legal work for the schools when he was around 35. He was elected to the school board at age 40. At age 50, when he had amassed a fortune, he started his own enterprise to build and to run model schools. He is, however, still working nearly full-time as the lead counsel in the company he helped found as a young lawyer.

There is another reason to develop a second major interest, and to develop it early. No one can expect to live very long without experiencing a serious setback in his or her life or work. There is the competent engineer who is passed over for promotion at age 45. There is the competent college professor who realizes at age 42 that she will never get a professorship at a big university, even though she may be fully qualified for it. There are tragedies in one's family life: the breakup of one's marriage or the loss of a child. At such times, a second major interest—not just a hobby—may make all the difference. The engineer, for example, now knows that he has not been very successful in his job. But in his outside activity—as church treasurer, for example—he is a success. One's family may break up, but in that outside activity there is still a community.

In a society in which success has become so terribly important, having options will become increasingly vital. Historically, there was no such thing as "success." The overwhelming majority of people did not expect anything but to stay in their "proper station," as an old English prayer has it. The only mobility was downward mobility.

In a knowledge society, however, we expect everyone to be a success. This is clearly an impossibility. For a great many people, there is at best an absence of failure. Wherever there is success, there has to be failure. And then it is vitally important for the individual, and equally for the individual's family, to have an area in which he or she can contribute, make a difference, and be *somebody*. That means finding a second area—whether in a second career, a parallel career, or a social venture—that offers an opportunity for being a leader, for being respected, for being a success.

The challenges of managing oneself may seem obvious, if not elementary. And the answers may seem self-evident to the point of appearing naïve. But managing oneself requires new and unprecedented things from the individual, and especially from the knowledge worker. In effect, managing oneself demands that each knowledge worker think and behave like a chief executive officer. Further, the shift from manual workers who do as they are told

There is one prerequisite for managing the second half of your life: You must begin doing so long before you enter it.

to knowledge workers who have to manage themselves profoundly challenges social structure. Every existing society, even the most individualistic one, takes two things for granted, if only subconsciously: that organizations outlive workers, and that most people stay put.

But today the opposite is true. Knowledge workers outlive organizations, and they are mobile. The need to manage oneself is therefore creating a revolution in human affairs.

Reprint R0501K
To order, see the next page
or call 800-988-0886 or 617-783-7500
or go to www.hbr.org

Managing Oneself

Further Reading

ARTICLES

The Post-Capitalist Executive: An Interview with Peter F. Drucker
by T. George Harris
Harvard Business Review
May–June 1993
Product no. 93302

Drucker explores the importance of self-management in the world of work. Corporations once built to last like the pyramids are now more like tents, he says. Thus individuals need to take responsibility for their own careers. Instead of assuming a traditional career trajectory up the corporate ladder, think in terms of a succession of professional assignments or projects.

In today's organizations, competence is measured less in terms of subject matter and more in terms of abilities—for example, empathy and stamina under pressure. So it's up to you to help others understand what you're able to contribute to the overall project.

Drucker also notes that your role as an executive or manager has changed. You no longer manage a workforce; you manage individuals with a variety of skills. Your job, then, is to combine these skills in a variety of configurations to create the best results for your company.

How to Play to Your Strengths
by Laura Morgan Roberts,
Gretchen Spreitzer, Jane Dutton,
Robert Quinn, Emily Heaphy, and
Brianna Barker
Harvard Business Review
January 2005
Product no. R0501G

Like Drucker, the authors of this article emphasize the importance of understanding and leveraging your strengths. They present a feedback tool called the Reflective Best Self (RBS) exercise, which offers a feedback experience distinct from performance reviews (that typically focus on problem areas). RBS enables you to tap into talents you may not be aware of and use them to enhance your career potential.

To begin the exercise, solicit comments from family, friends, colleagues, and teachers—asking for specific examples of times when your unique strengths generated especially important benefits. Next, search for common themes among the feedback, organizing them in a table to develop a clear picture of your strong suits. Then write a self-portrait: a description of yourself that distills what you've learned from your feedback. Finally, redesign your personal job description so you can better shape the positions you choose to play—both now and in the next phase of your career.

Harvard Business Review ⬩

To Order

For *Harvard Business Review* reprints and subscriptions, call 800-988-0886 or 617-783-7500. Go to www.hbr.org

For customized and quantity orders of *Harvard Business Review* article reprints, call 617-783-7626, or e-mail customizations@hbsp.harvard.edu

A CEO must be the steward of a living strategy that defines what the firm is and what it will become.

Putting Leadership Back into Strategy

by Cynthia A. Montgomery

Reprint R0801C

A CEO must be the steward of a living strategy that defines what the firm is and what it will become.

Putting Leadership Back into Strategy

by Cynthia A. Montgomery

Strategy is not what it used to be—or what it could be. In the past 25 years it has been presented, and we have come to think of it, as an analytical problem to be solved, a left-brain exercise of sorts. This perception, combined with strategy's high stakes, has led to an era of specialists—legions of MBAs and strategy consultants—armed with frameworks and techniques, eager to help managers analyze their industries or position their firms for strategic advantage.

This way of thinking about strategy has generated substantial benefits. We now know far more than before about the role market forces play in industry profitability and the importance of differentiating a firm from its competitors. These gains have come in large part from the infusion of economics into the study of strategy. That merger added much-needed theory and empirical evidence to strategy's underpinnings, providing considerable rigor and substance. But the benefits have not come without costs. A host of unintended consequences have developed from

what in its own right could be a very good thing. Most notably, strategy has been narrowed to a competitive game plan, divorcing it from a firm's larger sense of purpose; the CEO's unique role as arbiter and steward of strategy has been eclipsed; and the exaggerated emphasis on sustainable competitive advantage has drawn attention away from the fact that strategy must be a dynamic tool for guiding the development of a company over time.

To redress these issues, we need to think about strategy in a new way—one that recognizes the inherently fluid nature of competition and the attendant need for continuous, not periodic, leadership.

The Road to Here

Fifty years ago strategy was taught as part of the general management curriculum in business schools. In the academy as well as in practice, it was identified as the most important duty of the chief executive officer—the person with overarching responsibility for setting a company's course and seeing the journey through. This vital role encompassed both formulation and implementation: thinking and doing combined.

Although strategy had considerable breadth then, it didn't have much rigor. The ubiquitous SWOT model taught managers to assess a company's internal *strengths* and *weaknesses* and the *opportunities* and *threats* in its external environment, but the tools for doing so were pedestrian by any measure.

Advances over the next few decades not only refined the tools but spawned a new industry around strategy. Corporate-planning departments emerged and introduced formal systems and standards for strategic analysis. Consulting firms added their own frameworks, among them the Boston Consulting Group's influential growth-share matrix and McKinsey's 7-S framework. Academics weighed in, unleashing the power of economic analysis on problems of strategy and competition.

It has been a heady period, and the strategy tool kit is far richer because of it. That said, something has been lost along the way. While gaining depth, strategy has lost breadth and stature. It has become more about formulation than implementation, and more about getting the idea right at the outset than living with a strategy over time.

The teaching of strategy has both led and followed suit. At many top business schools, general management departments have been replaced by strategy groups made up of experts who delve into the economics of competitive advantage but rarely acknowledge the unique role leaders play in the process of formulating and implementing strategy. When the head of the strategy group at one major business school was asked recently to describe the common denominator among faculty members in his department, he replied, "We are a group of economists with a lively interest in business." An honest man and a telling comment.

Pulled apart and set on its own in this way, strategy both gains and loses. In terms of analytical precision, it is a big plus; organizationally, it is not. What we have lost sight of is that strategy is not just a plan, not just an idea; it is a way of life for a company. Strategy doesn't just position a firm in its external landscape; it defines what a firm will be.

Watching over strategy day in and day out is not only a CEO's greatest opportunity to outwit the competition; it is also his or her greatest opportunity to shape the firm itself.

Strategy and Being

In "How to Evaluate Corporate Strategy," an article that appeared in this magazine in 1963, the Harvard Business School lecturer Seymour Tilles proposed that of all the questions a chief executive is required to answer, one predominates: What kind of company do you want yours to be? He elaborated:

> If you ask young men what they want to accomplish by the time they are 40, the answers you get fall into two distinct categories. There are those—the great majority—who will respond in terms of what they want to *have*. This is especially true of graduate students of business administration. There are some men, however, who will answer in terms of the kind of men they hope to *be*. These are the only ones who have a clear idea of where they are going.
>
> The same is true of companies. For far too many companies, what little thinking goes on about the future is done primarily in money terms. There is nothing wrong with financial planning. Most companies should do more of it. But there is a basic fallacy in confusing a financial plan with thinking about the kind of company you want yours to become. It is like saying, "When I'm 40, I'm going to be *rich*." It leaves too many basic questions unanswered. Rich in what way? Rich doing what?

As strategy has striven to become a science, we have allowed this fundamental point to slip away. We need to reinstate it.

In 1996 Adam Brandenburger and Barry Nalebuff got close to this idea in their book *Co-opetition*, which recognized that in order to *claim* value, firms must first *create* value. This requires bringing something new to the world, something customers want that is different from or better than what others are providing.

To press their point, Brandenburger and Nalebuff urged managers to consider the world with their firm versus the world without it. The difference (if there is one) is the firm's unique added value—what would be lost to the world if the firm disappeared. Tilles might have described this as the firm's purpose, or its raison d'être. To say that a firm

Cynthia A. Montgomery is the Timken Professor of Business Administration and head of the strategy unit at Harvard Business School in Boston.

should have a clear sense of purpose may sound exceedingly philosophical. It is in fact exceedingly practical.

In the strategy portion of the Owner/President Management executive program at Harvard Business School, the notion of added value is core to everything we do. Early in the module, executives are asked to respond to the following questions:

• If your company were shuttered, to whom would it matter and why?

• Which of your customers would miss you the most and why?

• How long would it take for another firm to step into that void?

When the questions are presented, classrooms that minutes earlier were bursting with conversation fall silent—not because the questions are complex but because they are so basic and yet so difficult. Managers long accustomed to describing their companies by the industries they are in and the products they make often find themselves unable to say what is truly distinctive about their firms. For these leaders the challenge is a matter not of unearthing an existing purpose but of forging one.

The questions are as relevant to large multibusiness companies as they are to focused owner-led ones. As private equity firms proliferate and supply chains open up around the world, nothing is more important for complex corporate entities than a clear sense of purpose, a clear sense of why they matter. A board chairman at one such firm made the point bluntly when he asked, "What hot dish is this company bringing to the table?" He was issuing the same challenge.

Sam Palmisano, the CEO of IBM, is well aware of the importance of this sort of reflection. In 2003 he hosted a 72-hour online Values Jam in which he asked IBM's nearly 320,000 employees to weigh in on these questions: If our company disappeared tonight, how different would the world be tomorrow? Is there something about our company that makes a unique contribution to the world? (See "Leading Change When Business Is Good," HBR December 2004.)

In my experience, few leaders allow themselves to think about strategy at this level.

Purpose should be at the heart of strategy. It should give direction to every part of the firm—from the corporate office to the loading dock—and define the nature of the work that must be done. In "Unleashing the Power of Learning," a 1997 interview with HBR, John Browne, then the CEO of British Petroleum, put it this way: "A business has to have a clear purpose. If the purpose is not crystal clear, people in the business will not understand what kind of knowledge is critical and what they have to learn in order to improve performance….What do we mean by *purpose*? Our purpose is who we are and what makes us distinctive. It's what we as a company exist to achieve, and what we're willing and not willing to do to achieve it."

The most viable statements of purpose are easy to grasp and true to a company's distinctiveness. Pixar, one of the world's most innovative animation firms, says that it exists "to combine proprietary technology and world-class creative talent to develop computer-animated feature films with memorable characters and heartwarming stories that appeal to audiences of all ages." No films for mature audiences only. Lots of pushing the envelope. And who wouldn't recognize IKEA's intent to offer customers "a wide range of well-designed, functional home furnishing products at prices so low that as many people as possible will be able to afford them"? Sitting at the hub of the strategy wheel, purpose aligns all the functional pieces and draws the company into a logically consistent whole. Well understood, it serves as both a constraint on activity and a guide to behavior. As Michael Porter has argued, an effective strategy says not only what a firm will do but also, implicitly, what it will not do.

Forging a compelling organizational purpose is a close corporate equivalent to soul-searching. It does require the kind of careful analysis and left-brain thinking that MBAs have honed for a generation. Equally important to the task, however, is the right-brain activity in which managers are almost universally less well schooled. Creativity and insight are key, as is the ability to make judgments about a host of issues that can't be resolved through analysis alone.

Articulating and tending to a purpose-driven strategy so that it fills this role is no easy task. It is a human endeavor in the deepest sense of the term. Keeping all the parts of a company in proper balance while moving the enterprise forward is extraordinarily difficult. Even when they have substantial talent and a deep appreciation for the job, some CEOs ultimately don't get it right. Their legacies serve as sobering reminders of the complexities and the responsibilities of stewardship. (Witness BP's recent travails—the deficiencies in investments and operating practices that compromised workers' safety, threatened the environment, and contributed to Browne's abrupt departure from the company in 2007.) On the other hand, it is exactly these challenges that make the triumphs so rewarding.

Strategy and the Strategist
In most popular portrayals the strategist's job would seem to be finished once a carefully articulated strategy has been made ready for implementation. The idea has been formed, the next steps specified, the problem solved. But don't be fooled. The job of the strategist never ends. No matter how compelling a strategy is, or how clearly defined, it is unlikely to be a sufficient guide for a firm that aspires to a long and prosperous life.

Just as complete contracts are difficult to write with one's trading partners, so too complete strategies are difficult to specify in all their particulars. There will always be some choices that are not obvious. There will always be countless contingencies, good and bad, that cannot be fully anticipated. There will always be limits to communication and mutual understanding. As Oscar Wilde quipped, "Only the shallow know themselves." At heart, most strategies, like most people, involve some mystery.

Interpreting that mystery is an abiding responsibility of the chief strategist, the CEO. Sometimes this entails clarifying a point or helping an organization translate an idea into practice, such as what "best in class" will mean in that company and how it will be measured. Other times it entails much more: refashioning an element of the strategy, adding a previously missing piece, or reconsidering a commitment that no longer serves the company well. Whether you call this strategy implementation or strategy reformulation (the boundaries blur), it is arduous work and can't be separated from leadership of the firm.

Ryanair provides a case in point. During its early years the Irish airline entered the Dublin–London market with full service priced at less than half the fares of incumbents British Airways and Aer Lingus. Ryanair's leaders didn't anticipate the ferocity with which its competitors would respond. When the resulting fare war brought Ryanair to its knees, its leaders didn't simply urge the airline to try harder. They revamped the strategy and transformed the company into a no-frills player with a true low-cost business model. This involved changing the airline's fleet as well as its cost, fare, and route structures. "Yes, Aer Lingus attacked us," Michael O'Leary, Ryanair's CEO since 1994, has said, "but we exposed ourselves." Reborn, Ryanair went on to become a major airline and one of the world's most profitable.

When confronted with challenges, the CEO must recognize the strategic significance of issues being raised and opportunities being contemplated and see them through the lens of the whole, even as those with narrower responsibilities may be seeing the same issues parochially. While faithfully translating purpose into practice, the CEO must also remain open to the idea that the purpose itself may

The Missing Dimension

Over the past few decades strategy has become a plan that positions a company in its external landscape. That's not enough. Strategy should also guide the development of the company—its identity and purpose—over time.

The Prevailing Approach: **Strategy as a Set Solution**		What Is Missing: **Strategy as a Dynamic Process**
A long-term sustainable competitive advantage	Goal	Creation of value
The CEO and strategy consultants	Leadership	CEO as chief strategist; the job cannot be outsourced
Unchanging plan that derives from an analytical, left-brain exercise	Form	Organic process that is adaptive, holistic, and open-ended
Intense period of formulation followed by prolonged period of implementation	Time Frame	Everyday, continuous, unending
Defending an established strategy through time	Ongoing Activity	Fostering competitive advantages and developing the company through time

need to change. The judgments made at these moments of transition can make or break a leader or a firm.

Lou Gerstner, Palmisano's legendary predecessor, faced such a moment when he became CEO of a troubled IBM in 1993. To resurrect the company, he concluded, a radical shift in its mind-set was necessary. This required taking a fearless moral inventory of the business, realistically evaluating the firm's core capabilities, and shedding everything else. After making this assessment, Gerstner announced that IBM would no longer concern itself with the invention of technology but instead would focus on application. The company would move beyond its long history of creating computer hardware in order to provide integrated information technology services and solutions. "History," Gerstner has written, "shows that truly great and successful companies go through constant and sometimes difficult self-renewal of the base business."

The CEO is the one who chooses a company's identity, who has responsibility for declining certain opportunities and pursuing others. In this sense he or she serves as the guardian of organizational purpose, watching over the entity, guiding its course, bringing it back to the center time and time again, even as the center itself evolves.[1] This is why the job of the strategist cannot be outsourced. This is why the job of the strategist is never done, and why the vigil the CEO keeps must be a constant one.

Strategy and Becoming

What, after all, is the strategist trying to achieve? The conventional wisdom would say a sustainable long-term competitive advantage. I challenge this view. Although critically important, competitive advantage is not the ultimate goal. That way of thinking mistakes the means for the end and sends managers off on an unachievable quest.

Competitive advantage is essential to strategy. But it is only part of a bigger story, one frame in a motion picture. The very notion that there is a strategic holy grail—a strategy brilliantly conceived, carefully implemented, and valiantly defended through time—is dangerous. It is akin to the complete-contract view, in which all the thinking is done at the beginning and the key job of the strategist is to get that analysis right. If this were so, the role of the strategist would be limited and easy to separate from the leadership of a firm. If this were so, the strategist wouldn't have to be concerned with how the organization gets from here to there—the execution challenge writ large—or how it will capitalize on the learning it accumulates along the way.

But this is not so. Great firms—Toyota, Nike, and General Electric, to name a few—evolve and change. So do great strategies. This is not to say that continuity has no value. It is not to say that great resources and great advantages aren't built over the long term. It is, however, to acknowledge that the world, both inside and outside the firm, changes not only in big, discontinuous leaps but in frequent, smaller ones as well.

An ancient Greek legend provides a powerful metaphor for this process. According to the legend, the ship that the hero Theseus sailed back to Athens after slaying the Minotaur in Crete was rebuilt over time, plank by plank. As each plank decayed, it was replaced by another, until every plank in the ship had been changed. Was it then still the same ship? If not, at what point—with which plank—did the ship's identity shift?

This metaphor captures the evolution of most companies. Corporate identities are changed not only by cataclysmic restructurings and grand pronouncements but also by decision after decision, year after year, captain after captain. An organic conception of strategy recognizes that whatever constitutes strategic advantage will eventually change. It recognizes the difference between defending a firm's added value as established at any given moment and ensuring that a firm is adding value over time. Holding too strongly to one competitive advantage or one purpose may result in the firm's being controlled by a perception of value long after that value has diminished in significance. It encourages managers to see their strategies as set in concrete and, when spotting trouble ahead, to go into defensive mode, hunkering down and protecting the status quo.

Apple Computer was caught in this trap for most of the 1990s. The company stubbornly stuck to its original strategy of producing high-end differentiated personal computers, convinced that it was adding value even as the intensely competitive marketplace told it otherwise. By the summer of 1997 Apple's share

The need to create and re-create reasons for a company's continued existence sets the strategist apart from every other individual in the company.

price was at a 10-year low, its market share had plummeted to about 3%, and industry pundits were trumpeting the company's demise. The strategy had performed so poorly that there was little left to defend. Only after Steve Jobs returned as CEO, reclaimed the best of what Apple once was (a passionate design company that believed technology could change the world), and took the firm into new businesses (digital audio players, cell phones, and retailing) with distinctive products did the company attract a new mass of passionately loyal customers and generate handsome returns. Plank by plank the company changed its identity while remaining in many respects the same. Fittingly, in January 2007 it dropped "Computer" from its name and became simply Apple Inc.

The need to create and re-create reasons for a company's continued existence sets the strategist apart from every other individual in

the company. He or she must keep one eye on how the company is currently adding value and the other eye on changes, both inside and outside the company, that either threaten its position or present some new opportunity for adding value. Guiding this never-ending process, bringing perspective to the midst of action and purpose to the flow—not solving the strategy puzzle once—is the crowning responsibility of the CEO.

1. Kenneth R. Andrews, in *The Concept of Corporate Strategy* (Irwin, 1971), described one of the roles of the CEO as the "architect of organization purpose." I prefer the term "guardian of organizational purpose," because it encompasses both formulation and implementation, and because it implies a more ongoing responsibility.

Reprint R0801C
To order, see the next page
or call 800-988-0886 or 617-783-7500
or go to www.hbrreprints.org

Further Reading

Harvard Business Review ♛

Harvard Business Review ⬡

www.hbrreprints.org

Leaders are made, not born, and how they develop is critical for organizational change.

Seven Transformations of Leadership

by David Rooke and William R. Torbert

Included with this full-text *Harvard Business Review* article:

Seven Transformations of Leadership

The Idea in Brief

Every company needs transformational leaders—those who spearhead changes that elevate profitability, expand market share, and change the rules of the game in their industry. But few executives understand the unique strengths needed to become such a leader. Result? They miss the opportunity to develop those strengths. They and their firms lose out.

How to avoid this scenario? Recognize that great leaders are differentiated not by their personality or philosophy but by their **action logic**—how they interpret their own and others' behavior and how they maintain power or protect against threats.

Some leaders rely on action logics that hinder organizational performance. Opportunists, for example, believe in winning any way possible, and often exploit others to score personal gains. Few people follow them for long. Other types prove potent change agents. In particular, Strategists believe that every aspect of their organization is open to discussion and transformation. Their action logic enables them to challenge perceptions that constrain their organizations and to overcome resistance to change. They create compelling, shared visions and lead the pragmatic initiatives needed to realize those visions.

Though Strategists are rare, you *can* develop their defining strengths. How? Diagnose your current action logic and work to upgrade it. The payoff? You help your company execute the changes it needs to excel.

The Idea in Practice

SEVEN TYPES OF ACTION LOGIC

Type	Characteristics	Strengths	Weaknesses
Opportunist	*Wins any way possible.* Self-oriented; manipulative; "might makes right."	Good in emergencies and in pursuing sales.	Few people want to follow them for the long term.
Diplomat	*Avoids conflict.* Wants to belong; obeys group norms; doesn't rock the boat.	Supportive glue on teams.	Can't provide painful feedback or make the hard decisions needed to improve performance.
Expert	*Rules by logic and expertise.* Uses hard data to gain consensus and buy-in.	Good individual contributor.	Lacks emotional intelligence; lacks respect for those with less expertise.
Achiever	*Meets strategic goals.* Promotes teamwork; juggles managerial duties and responds to market demands to achieve goals.	Well suited to managerial work.	Inhibits thinking outside the box.
Individualist	*Operates in unconventional ways.* Ignores rules he/she regards as irrelevant.	Effective in venture and consulting roles.	Irritates colleagues and bosses by ignoring key organizational processes and people.
Strategist	*Generates organizational and personal change.* Highly collaborative; weaves visions with pragmatic, timely initiatives; challenges existing assumptions.	Generates transformations over the short and long term.	None
Alchemist	*Generates social transformations (e.g., Nelson Mandela).* Reinvents organizations in historically significant ways.	Leads societywide change.	None

CHANGING YOUR ACTION LOGIC TYPE

To change your action logic type, experiment with new interpersonal behaviors, forge new kinds of relationships, and seize advantage of work opportunities. For example:

The Idea in Practice (continued)

To advance from. . .	Take these steps
Expert to Achiever	Focus more on delivering results than on perfecting your knowledge: • Become aware of differences between your assumptions and those of others. For example, practice new conversational strategies such as "You may be right, but I'd like to understand what leads you to believe that." • Participate in training programs on topics such as effective delegation and leading high-performing teams
Achiever to Individualist	Instead of accepting goals as givens to be achieved: • Reflect on the worth of the goals themselves, with the aim of improving future goals • Use annual leadership development planning to thoughtfully set the highest-impact goals
Individualist to Strategist	Engage in peer-to-peer development: • Establish mutual mentoring with members of your professional network (board members, top managers, industry leaders) who can challenge your assumptions and practices, as well as those of your company and industry. Example: One CEO of a dental hygiene company envisioned introducing affordable dental hygiene in developing countries. He explored the idea with colleagues across the country, eventually proposing an educational and charitable venture that his parent company agreed to fund. He was promoted to a new vice presidency for international ventures within the parent company.

Leaders are made, not born, and how they develop is critical for organizational change.

Seven Transformations of Leadership

by David Rooke and William R. Torbert

Most developmental psychologists agree that what differentiates leaders is not so much their philosophy of leadership, their personality, or their style of management. Rather, it's their internal "action logic"—how they interpret their surroundings and react when their power or safety is challenged. Relatively few leaders, however, try to understand their own action logic, and fewer still have explored the possibility of changing it.

They should, because we've found that leaders who do undertake a voyage of personal understanding and development can transform not only their own capabilities but also those of their companies. In our close collaboration with psychologist Susanne Cook-Greuter—and our 25 years of extensive survey-based consulting at companies such as Deutsche Bank, Harvard Pilgrim Health Care, Hewlett-Packard, NSA, Trillium Asset Management, Aviva, and Volvo—we've worked with thousands of executives as they've tried to develop their leadership skills. The good news is that leaders who make an effort to understand their own action logic can improve their ability to lead. But to do that, it's important first to understand what kind of leader you already are.

The Seven Action Logics

Our research is based on a sentence-completion survey tool called the Leadership Development Profile. Using this tool, participants are asked to complete 36 sentences that begin with phrases such as "A good leader...," to which responses vary widely:

"...cracks the whip."

"...realizes that it's important to achieve good performance from subordinates."

"...juggles competing forces and takes responsibility for her decisions."

By asking participants to complete sentences of this type, it's possible for highly trained evaluators to paint a picture of how participants interpret their own actions and the world around them; these "pictures" show which one of seven developmental action logics—Opportunist, Diplomat, Expert, Achiever, Individualist, Strategist, or Alchemist—currently functions as a leader's dominant way of thinking. Leaders can move through these categories as their abilities grow, so taking the Leadership Development Profile again several years later can reveal whether a leader's action logic has evolved.

Over the past 25 years, we and other researchers have administered the sentence-completion survey to thousands of managers and professionals, most between the ages of 25 and 55, at hundreds of American and European companies (as well as nonprofits and governmental agencies) in diverse industries. What we found is that the levels of corporate and individual performance vary according to action logic. Notably, we found that the three types of leaders associated with below-average corporate performance (Opportunists, Diplomats, and Experts) accounted for 55% of our sample. They were significantly less effective at implementing organizational strategies than the 30% of the sample who measured as Achievers. Moreover, only the final 15% of managers in the sample (Individualists, Strategists, and Alchemists) showed the consistent capacity to innovate and to successfully transform their organizations.

To understand how leaders fall into such distinct categories and corporate performance, let's look in more detail at each leadership style in turn, starting with the least productive (and least complex).

The Opportunist

Our most comforting finding was that only 5% of the leaders in our sample were characterized by mistrust, egocentrism, and manipulativeness. We call these leaders Opportunists, a title that reflects their tendency to focus on personal wins and see the world and other people as opportunities to be exploited. Their approach to the outside world is largely determined by their perception of control—in other words, how they will react to an event depends primarily on whether or not they think they can direct the outcome. They treat other people as objects or as competitors who are also out for themselves.

Opportunists tend to regard their bad behavior as legitimate in the cut and thrust of an eye-for-an-eye world. They reject feedback, externalize blame, and retaliate harshly. One can see this action logic in the early work of Larry

Ellison (now CEO of Oracle). Ellison describes his managerial style at the start of his career as "management by ridicule." "You've got to be good at intellectual intimidation and rhetorical bullying," he once told Matthew Symonds of the *Economist*. "I'd excuse my behavior by telling myself I was just having 'an open and honest debate.' The fact is, I just didn't know any better."

Few Opportunists remain managers for long, unless they transform to more effective action logics (as Ellison has done). Their constant firefighting, their style of self-aggrandizement, and their frequent rule breaking is the antithesis of the kind of leader people want to work with for the long term. If you have worked for an Opportunist, you will almost certainly remember it as a difficult time. By the same token, corporate environments that breed opportunism seldom endure, although Opportunists often survive longer than they should because they provide an exciting environment in which younger executives, especially, can take risks. As one ex-Enron senior staffer said, "Before the fall, those were such exciting years. We felt we could do anything, pull off everything, write our own rules. The pace was wild, and we all just rode it." Of course, Enron's shareholders and pensioners would reasonably feel that they were paying too heavily for that staffer's adventure.

The Diplomat

The Diplomat makes sense of the world around him in a more benign way than the Opportunist does, but this action logic can also have extremely negative repercussions if the leader is a senior manager. Loyally serving the group, the Diplomat seeks to please higher-status colleagues while avoiding conflict. This action logic is focused on gaining control of one's own behavior—more than on gaining control of external events or other people. According to the Diplomat's action logic, a leader gains more enduring acceptance and influence by cooperating with group norms and by performing his daily roles well.

In a support role or a team context, this type of executive has much to offer. Diplomats provide social glue to their colleagues and ensure that attention is paid to the needs of others, which is probably why the great majority of Diplomats work at the most junior rungs of management, in jobs such as

David Rooke (david@harthill.co.uk) is a partner at Harthill Consulting in Hewelsfield, England. **William R. Torbert** (torbert@bc.edu) is a professor at Boston College's Carroll School of Management in Massachusetts. They are coauthors of *Action Inquiry: The Secret of Timely and Transforming Leadership* (Berrett-Koehler, 2004).

frontline supervisor, customer service representative, or nurse practitioner. Indeed, research into 497 managers in different industries showed that 80% of all Diplomats were at junior levels. By contrast, 80% of all Strategists were at senior levels, suggesting that

managers who grow into more effective action logics—like that of the Strategist—have a greater chance of being promoted.

Diplomats are much more problematic in top leadership roles because they try to ignore conflict. They tend to be overly polite and

Seven Ways of Leading

Different leaders exhibit different kinds of action logic—ways in which they interpret their surroundings and react when their power or safety is challenged. In our research of thousands of leaders, we observed seven types of action logics. The least effec- tive for organizational leadership are the Opportunist and Diplomat; the most effec- tive, the Strategist and Alchemist. Knowing your own action logic can be the first step toward developing a more effective leader- ship style. If you recognize yourself as an In- dividualist, for example, you can work, through both formal and informal mea- sures, to develop the strengths and characteristics of a Strategist.

Action Logic	Characteristics	Strengths	% of research sample profiling at this action logic
Opportunist	*Wins any way possible.* Self-oriented; manipulative, "might makes right."	Good in emergencies and in sales opportunities.	**5%**
Diplomat	*Avoids overt conflict.* Wants to belong; obeys group norms; rarely rocks the boat.	Good as supportive glue within an office; helps bring people together.	**12%**
Expert	*Rules by logic and expertise.* Seeks rational efficiency.	Good as an individual contributor.	**38%**
Achiever	*Meets strategic goals.* Effectively achieves goals through teams; juggles managerial duties and market demands.	Well suited to managerial roles; action and goal oriented.	**30%**
Individualist	*Interweaves competing personal and company action logics.* Creates unique structures to resolve gaps between strategy and performance.	Effective in venture and consulting roles.	**10%**
Strategist	*Generates organizational and personal transformations.* Exercises the power of mutual inquiry, vigilance, and vulnerability for both the short and long term.	Effective as a transforma- tional leader.	**4%**
Alchemist	*Generates social transformations.* Inte- grates material, spiritual, and societal transformation.	Good at leading society-wide transformations.	**1%**

friendly and find it virtually impossible to give challenging feedback to others. Initiating change, with its inevitable conflicts, represents a grave threat to the Diplomat, and he will avoid it if at all possible, even to the point of self-destruction.

Consider one Diplomat who became the interim CEO of an organization when his predecessor died suddenly from an aneurysm. When the board split on the selection of a permanent successor, it asked the Diplomat to carry on. Our Diplomat relished his role as a ceremonial figurehead and was a sought-after speaker at public events. Unfortunately, he found the more conflictual requirements of the job less to his liking. He failed, for instance, to replace a number of senior managers who had serious ongoing performance issues and were resisting the change program his predecessor had initiated. Because the changes were controversial, the Diplomat avoided meetings, even planning business trips for the times when the senior team would meet. The team members were so frustrated by the Diplomat's attitude that they eventually resigned en masse. He "resolved" this crisis by thanking the team publicly for its contribution and appointing new team members. Eventually, in the face of mounting losses arising from this poor management, the board decided to demote the Diplomat to his former role as vice president.

The Expert

The largest category of leader is that of Experts, who account for 38% of all professionals in our sample. In contrast to Opportunists, who focus on trying to control the world around them, and Diplomats, who concentrate on controlling their own behavior, Experts try to exercise control by perfecting their knowledge, both in their professional and personal lives. Exercising watertight thinking is extremely important to Experts. Not surprisingly, many accountants, investment analysts, marketing researchers, software engineers, and consultants operate from the Expert action logic. Secure in their expertise, they present hard data and logic in their efforts to gain consensus and buy-in for their proposals.

Experts are great individual contributors because of their pursuit of continuous improvement, efficiency, and perfection. But as managers, they can be problematic because they are so completely sure they are right.

Initiating change, with its inevitable conflicts, represents a grave threat to the Diplomat, and he will avoid it if at all possible, even to the point of self-destruction.

When subordinates talk about a my-way-or-the-highway type of boss, they are probably talking about someone operating from an Expert action logic. Experts tend to view collaboration as a waste of time ("Not all meetings are a waste of time—some are canceled!"), and they will frequently treat the opinion of people less expert than themselves with contempt. Emotional intelligence is neither desired nor appreciated. As Sun Microsystems' CEO Scott McNealy put it: "I don't do feelings; I'll leave that to Barry Manilow."

It comes as no surprise, then, that after unsuccessfully pleading with him to scale back in the face of growing losses during the dot-com debacle of 2001 and 2002, nearly a dozen members of McNealy's senior management team left.

The Achiever

For those who hope someday to work for a manager who both challenges and supports them and creates a positive team and interdepartmental atmosphere, the good news is that a large proportion, 30%, of the managers in our research measured as Achievers. While these leaders create a positive work environment and focus their efforts on deliverables, the downside is that their style often inhibits thinking outside the box.

Achievers have a more complex and integrated understanding of the world than do managers who display the three previous action logics we've described. They're open to feedback and realize that many of the ambiguities and conflicts of everyday life are due to differences in interpretation and ways of relating. They know that creatively transforming or resolving clashes requires sensitivity to relationships and the ability to influence others in positive ways. Achievers can also reliably lead a team to implement new strategies over a one-to three-year period, balancing immediate and long-term objectives. One study of ophthalmologists in private practice showed that those who scored as Achievers had lower staff turnover, delegated more responsibility, and had practices that earned at least twice the gross annual revenues of those run by Experts.

Achievers often find themselves clashing with Experts. The Expert subordinate, in particular, finds the Achiever leader hard to take because he cannot deny the reality of the Achiever's success even though he feels superior. Consider Hewlett-Packard, where the research engineers tend to score as Experts and the lab managers as higher-level Achievers. At one project meeting, a lab manager—a decided Achiever—slammed her coffee cup on the table and exclaimed, "I *know* we can get 18 features into this, but the customers want delivery some time this century, and the main eight features will do." "Philistine!" snorted one engineer, an Expert. But this kind of conflict isn't always destructive. In fact, it provides much of the fuel that has ignited—and sustained—the competitiveness of many of the country's most successful corporations.

The Individualist

The Individualist action logic recognizes that neither it nor any of the other action logics are "natural"; all are constructions of oneself and the world. This seemingly abstract idea enables the 10% of Individualist leaders to contribute unique practical value to their organizations; they put personalities and ways of relating into perspective and communicate well with people who have other action logics.

What sets Individualists apart from Achievers is their awareness of a possible conflict between their principles and their actions, or between the organization's values and its implementation of those values. This conflict becomes the source of tension, creativity, and a growing desire for further development.

Individualists also tend to ignore rules they regard as irrelevant, which often makes them a source of irritation to both colleagues and bosses. "So, what do you think?" one of our clients asked us as he was debating whether to let go of one of his star performers, a woman who had been measured as an Individualist. Sharon (not her real name) had been asked to set up an offshore shared service function in the Czech Republic in order to provide IT support to two separate and internally competitive divisions operating there. She formed a highly cohesive team within budget and so far ahead of schedule that she quipped that she was "delivering services before Group Business Risk had delivered its report saying it can't be done."

The trouble was that Sharon had a reputation within the wider organization as a wild card. Although she showed great political savvy when it came to her individual projects, she put many people's noses out of joint in the larger organization because of her unique, unconventional ways of operating. Eventually, the CEO was called in (not for the first time) to resolve a problem created by her failure to acknowledge key organizational processes and people who weren't on her team.

Many of the dynamics created by different action logics are illustrated by this story and its outcome. The CEO, whose own action logic was that of an Achiever, did not see how he could challenge Sharon to develop and move beyond creating such problems. Although ambivalent about her, he decided to retain her because she was delivering and because the organization had recently lost several capable, if unconventional, managers.

So Sharon stayed, but only for a while. Eventually, she left the company to set up an offshoring consultancy. When we examine in the second half of this article how to help executives transform their leadership action logics, we'll return to this story to see how both Sharon and the CEO might have succeeded in transforming theirs.

The Strategist

Strategists account for just 4% of leaders. What sets them apart from Individualists is their focus on organizational constraints and perceptions, which they treat as discussable and transformable. Whereas the Individualist masters communication with colleagues who have different action logics, the Strategist masters the second-order organizational impact of actions and agreements. The Strategist is also adept at creating shared visions across different action logics—visions that encourage both personal and organizational transformations. According to the Strategist's action logic, organizational and social change is an iterative developmental process that requires awareness and close leadership attention.

Strategists deal with conflict more comfortably than do those with other action logics, and they're better at handling people's instinctive resistance to change. As a result, Strategists are highly effective change agents. We found confirmation of this in our recent study of ten CEOs in six different industries. All of their organizations had the stated objective of transforming themselves and had engaged consultants to help with the process. Each CEO filled out a Leadership Development Profile, which showed that five of them were Strategists and the other five fell into other action logics. The Strategists succeeded in generating one or more organizational transformations over a four-year period; their companies' profitability, market share, and reputation all improved. By contrast, only two of the other five CEOs succeeded in transforming their organizations—despite help from consultants, who themselves profiled as Strategists.

Strategists are fascinated with three distinct levels of social interplay: personal relationships, organizational relations, and national and international developments. Consider Joan Bavaria, a CEO who, back in 1985, measured as a Strategist. Bavaria created one of the first socially responsible investment funds, a new subdivision of the investments industry, which by the end of 2001 managed more than $3 trillion in funds. In 1982, Bavaria founded Trillium Asset Management, a worker-owned company, which she still heads. She also cowrote the CERES Environmental Principles, which dozens of major companies have signed. In the late 1990s, CERES, working with the United Nations, created the Global Reporting Initiative, which supports financial, social, and environmental transparency and accountability worldwide.

Here we see the Strategist action logic at work. Bavaria saw a unique moment in which to make ethical investing a viable business, then established Trillium to execute her plan. Strategists typically have socially conscious business ideas that are carried out in a highly collaborative manner. They seek to weave together idealist visions with pragmatic, timely initiatives and principled actions. Bavaria worked beyond the boundaries of her own organization to influence the socially responsible investment industry as a whole and later made the development of social and environmental accountability standards an international endeavor by involving the United Nations. Many Achievers will use their influence to successfully promote their own companies. The Strategist works to create ethical principles and practices beyond the interests of herself or her organization.

The Alchemist

The final leadership action logic for which we have data and experience is the Alchemist. Our studies of the few leaders we have identified as Alchemists suggest that what sets them apart from Strategists is their ability to renew or even reinvent themselves and their organizations in historically significant ways. Whereas the Strategist will move from one engagement to another, the Alchemist has an extraordinary capacity to deal simultaneously with many situations at multiple levels. The Alchemist can talk with both kings and commoners. He can deal with immediate priorities yet never lose sight of long-term goals.

Alchemists constitute 1% of our sample, which indicates how rare it is to find them in business or anywhere else. Through an extensive search process, we found six Alchemists who were willing to participate in an up-close study of their daily actions. Though this is obviously a very small number that cannot statistically justify generalization, it's worth noting that all six Alchemists shared certain characteristics. On a daily basis, all were engaged in multiple organizations and found time to deal with issues raised by each. However, they were not in a constant rush—nor did they devote hours on end to a single activity. Alchemists are typically charismatic and extremely aware individuals who live by high moral standards. They focus intensely on the truth. Perhaps most important, they're able to catch unique moments in the history of their organizations, creating symbols and metaphors that speak to people's hearts and minds. In one conservative financial services company in the UK, a recently appointed CEO turned up for work in a tracksuit instead of his usual pinstripes but said nothing about it to anyone. People wondered whether this was a new dress code. Weeks later, the CEO spoke publicly about his attire and the need to be unconventional and to move with greater agility and speed.

A more celebrated example of an Alchemist is Nelson Mandela. Although we never formally profiled Mandela, he exemplifies the Alchemist action logic. In 1995, Mandela symbolized the unity of a new South Africa when he attended the Rugby World Cup game in which the Springboks, the South African national team, were playing. Rugby had been the bastion of white supremacy, but Mandela attended the game. He walked on to the pitch wearing the Springboks' jersey so hated by black South Africans, at the same time giving the clenched fist salute of the ANC, thereby appealing, almost impossibly, both to black and white South Africans. As Tokyo Sexwale, ANC activist and premier of South Africa's Gauteng prov-

What sets Alchemists apart from Strategists is their ability to renew or even reinvent themselves and their organizations in historically significant ways.

ince, said of him: "Only Mandela could wear an enemy jersey. Only Mandela would go down there and be associated with the Springboks... All the years in the underground, in the trenches, denial, self-denial, away from home, prison, it was worth it. That's all we wanted to see."

Evolving as a Leader

The most remarkable—and encouraging—finding from our research is that leaders can transform from one action logic to another. We have, in fact, documented a number of leaders who have succeeded in transforming themselves from Experts into Achievers, from Achievers into Individualists, and from Individualists into Strategists.

Take the case of Jenny, one of our clients, who initially measured as an Expert. She became disillusioned with her role in her company's PR department and resigned in order to, as she said, "sort out what I really want to do." Six months later, she joined a different company in a similar role, and two years after that we profiled her again and she still measured as an Expert. Her decision to resign from the first company, take a "sabbatical," and then join the second company had made no difference to her action logic. At that point, Jenny chose to join a group of peer leaders committed to examining their current leadership patterns and to experimenting with new ways of acting. This group favored the Strategist perspective (and the founder of the group was profiled as an Alchemist), which in the end helped Jenny's development. She learned that her habit of consistently taking a critical position, which she considered "usefully objective," isolated her and generated distrust. As a result of the peer group's feedback, she started a series of small and private experiments, such as asking questions rather than criticizing. She realized that instead of seeing the faults in others, she had to be clear about what *she* could contribute and, in doing so, started the move from an Expert to an Achiever. Spiritually, Jenny learned that she needed an ongoing community of inquiry at the center of her life and found a spiritual home for continuing reflection in Quaker meetings, which later supported (and indeed signaled) her transition from an Achiever to an Individualist.

Two years later, Jenny left the second job to start her own company, at which point she began profiling as a Strategist. This was a highly unusual movement of three action logics in such a short time. We have had only two other instances in which a leader has transformed twice in less than four years.

As Jenny's case illustrates, there are a number of personal changes that can support leadership transformation. Jenny experienced loss of faith in the system and feelings of boredom, irritability, burnout, depression, and even anger. She began to ask herself existential questions. But another indication of a leader's readiness to transform is an increasing attraction to the qualities she begins to intuit in people with more effective action logics. Jenny, as we saw, was drawn to and benefited hugely from her Strategist peer group as well as from a mentor who exhibited the Alchemist action logic. This search for new perspectives often manifests itself in personal transformations: The ready-to-transform leader starts developing new relationships. She may also explore new forms of spiritual practice or new forms of centering and self-expression, such as playing a musical instrument or doing tai chi.

External events can also trigger and support transformation. A promotion, for example, may give a leader the opportunity to expand his or her range of capabilities. Earlier, we cited the frustration of Expert research engineers at Hewlett-Packard with the product and delivery attitude of Achiever lab managers. Within a year of one engineer's promotion to lab manager, a role that required coordination of others and cooperation across departments, the former Expert was profiling as an Achiever. Although he initially took some heat ("Sellout!") from his former buddies, his new Achiever awareness meant that he was more focused on customers' needs and clearer about delivery schedules. For the first time, he understood the dance between engineers trying to perfect the technology and managers trying to deliver on budget and on schedule.

Changes to a manager's work practices and environment can also facilitate transformation. At one company we studied, leaders changed from Achievers to Individualists partly because of simple organizational and process changes. At the company's senior manager meetings, for example, executives other than the CEO had the chance to lead the meetings; these opportunities, which were supported by new spirit of openness, feedback, and frank debate, fostered professional growth among many of the company's leaders.

Planned and structured development interventions are another means of supporting leadership transformation. We worked with a leading oil and gas exploration company on developing the already high-level capabilities of a pool of future senior managers; the managers were profiled and then interviewed by two consultants who explored each manager's action logic and how it constrained and enabled him or her to perform current and recent roles. Challenges were discussed as well as a view of the individual's potential and a possible developmental plan. After the exercise, several managers, whose Individualist and Strategist capabilities had not been fully understood by the company, were appreciated and engaged differently in their roles. What's more, the organization's own definition of leadership talent was reframed to include the capabilities of the Individualist and Strategist action logics. This in turn demanded that the company radically revisit its competency framework to incorporate such expectations as "sees issues from multiple perspectives" and "creates deep change without formal power."

Now that we've looked generally at some of the changes and interventions that can support leadership development, let's turn to some specifics about how the most common transformations are apt to take place.

From Expert to Achiever

This transformation is the most commonly observed and practiced among businesspeople and by those in management and executive education. For the past generation or more, the training departments of large companies have been supporting the development of managers from Experts into Achievers by running programs with titles like "Management by Objectives," "Effective Delegation," and "Managing People for Results." These programs typically emphasize getting results through flexible strategies rather than through one right method used in one right way.

Observant leaders and executive coaches can also formulate well-structured exercises and questions related to everyday work to help Experts become aware of the different assumptions they and others may be making. These efforts can help Experts practice new conversational strategies such as, "You may be right,

but I'd like to understand what leads you to believe that." In addition, those wishing to push Experts to the next level should consider rewarding Achiever competencies like timely delivery of results, the ability to manage for performance, and the ability to implement strategic priorities.

Within business education, MBA programs are apt to encourage the development of the more pragmatic Achievers by frustrating the perfectionist Experts. The heavy workloads, use of multidisciplinary and ambiguous case studies, and teamwork requirements all promote the development of Achievers. By contrast, MSc programs, in particular disciplines such as finance or marketing research, tend to reinforce the Expert perspective.

Still, the transition from Expert to Achiever remains one of the most painful bottlenecks in most organizations. We've all heard the eternal lament of engineers, lawyers, and other professionals whose Expert success has saddled them with managerial duties, only to estrange them from the work they love. Their challenge becomes working as highly effective Achievers who can continue to use their in-depth expertise to succeed as leaders and managers.

From Achiever to Individualist

Although organizations and business schools have been relatively successful in developing leaders to the Achiever action logic, they have, with few exceptions, a dismal record in recognizing, supporting, and *actively* developing leaders to the Individualist and Strategist action logics, let alone to the Alchemist logic. This is not surprising. In many organizations, the Achiever, with his drive and focus on the endgame, is seen as the finish line for development: "This is a competitive industry—we need to keep a sharp focus on the bottom line."

The development of leaders beyond the Achiever action logic requires a very different tack from that necessary to bring about the Expert-to-Achiever transformation. Interventions must encourage self-awareness on the part of the evolving leader as well as a greater awareness of other worldviews. In both business and personal relationships, speaking and listening must come to be experienced not as necessary, taken-for-granted ways of communicating predetermined ideas but as intrinsically forward-thinking, creative actions. Achievers use inquiry to determine whether they (and the teams and organization to which they belong) are accomplishing their goals and how they might accomplish them more effectively. The developing Individualist, however, begins to inquire about and reflect on the goals themselves—with the aim of improving future goals. Annual development plans that set new goals, are generated through probing and trusting conversation, are actively supported through executive coaching, and are carefully reviewed at the end of the cycle can be critical enablers at this point. Yet few boards and CEOs appreciate how valuable this time investment can be, and it is all too easily sacrificed in the face of short-term objectives, which can seem more pressing to leaders whose action logics are less developed.

Let's go back to the case of Sharon, the Individualist we described earlier whose Achiever CEO wasn't able to manage her. How might a coach or consultant have helped the CEO feel less threatened by Sharon and more capable of supporting her development while also being more open to his own needs and potential? One way would have been to try role-playing, asking the CEO to play Sharon while the coach or consultant enacts the CEO role. The role-playing might have gone as follows:

"Sharon, I want to talk with you about your future here at our company. Your completion of the Czech project under budget and ahead of time is one more sign that you have the initiative, creativity, and determination to make the senior team here. At the same time, I've had to pick up a number of pieces after you that I shouldn't have had to. I'd like to brainstorm together about how you can approach future projects in a way that eliminates this hassle and gets key players on your side. Then, we can chat several times over the next year as you begin to apply whatever new principles we come up with. Does this seem like a good use of our time, or do you have a different perspective on the issue?"

Note that the consultant in the CEO's role offers clear praise, a clear description of a limitation, a proposed path forward, and an inquiry that empowers the CEO (playing Sharon) to reframe the dilemma if he wishes. Thus, instead of giving the CEO one-way advice about what he should do, the coach enacts a dialogic scenario with him, illustrating a new kind of practice and letting the CEO judge whether the enacted relationship is a positive one. The

point is not so much to teach the CEO a new conversational repertoire but to make him more comfortable with how the Individualist sees and makes sense of the world around her and what feedback may motivate her to commit to further learning. Such specific experiments with new ways of listening and talking can gradually dissolve the fears associated with transformational learning.

To Strategist and Beyond

Leaders who are moving toward the Strategist and Alchemist action logics are no longer primarily seeking personal skills that will make them more effective within existing organizational systems. They will already have mastered many of those skills. Rather, they are exploring the disciplines and commitments entailed in creating projects, teams, networks, strategic alliances, and whole organizations on the basis of collaborative inquiry. It is this ongoing practice of reframing inquiry that makes them and their corporations so successful.

The path toward the Strategist and Alchemist action logics is qualitatively different from other leadership development processes. For a start, emergent Strategists and Alchemists are no longer seeking mentors to help them sharpen existing skills and to guide them toward influential networks (although they may seek spiritual and ethical guidance from mentors). Instead, they are seeking to engage in mutual mentoring with peers who are already part of their networks (such as board members, top managers, or leaders within a scientific discipline). The objective of this senior-peer mentoring is not, in conventional terms, to increase the chances of success but to create a sustainable community of people who can challenge the emergent leader's assumptions and practices and those of his company, industry, or other area of activity.

We witnessed just this kind of peer-to-peer development when one senior client became concerned that he, his company, and the industry as a whole were operating at the Achiever level. This concern, of course, was itself a sign of his readiness to transform beyond that logic. This executive—the CEO of a dental hygiene company—and his company were among the most successful of the parent company's subsidiaries. However, realizing that he and those around him had been keeping their heads down, he chose to initiate a research project—

on introducing affordable dental hygiene in developing countries—that was decidedly out of the box for him and for the corporation.

The CEO's timing was right for such an initiative, and he used the opportunity to engage in collaborative inquiry with colleagues across the country. Eventually, he proposed an educational and charitable venture, which the parent company funded. The executive was promoted to a new vice presidency for international ventures within the parent company—a role he exercised with an increased sense of collaboration and a greater feeling of social responsibility for his company in emerging markets.

Formal education and development processes can also guide individuals toward a Strategist action logic. Programs in which participants act as leaders and challenge their conventional assumptions about leading and organizing are very effective. Such programs will be either long term (one or two years) or repeated, intense experiences that nurture the moment-to-moment awareness of participants, always providing the shock of dissonance that stimulates them to reexamine their worldviews. Path-breaking programs of this type can be found at a few universities and consultancies around the globe. Bath University in the UK, for instance, sponsors a two-year master's degree in responsibility and business practice in which students work together during six one-week get-togethers. These programs involve small-learning teams, autobiographical writing, psychodrama, deep experiences in nature, and a yearlong business project that involves action and reflection. Interestingly, many people who attend these programs report that these experiences have had the transformative power of a life-altering event, such as a career or existential crisis or a new marriage.

Leadership Teams and Leadership Cultures Within Organizations

So far, our discussion has focused on the leadership styles of individuals. But we have found that our categories of leadership styles can be used to describe teams and organizations as well. Here we will talk briefly about the action logics of teams.

Over the long term, the most effective teams are those with a Strategist culture, in which the group sees business challenges as opportunities for growth and learning on the part of both individuals and the organization. A leadership team at one of the companies we worked with decided to invite managers from across departments to participate in time-to-market new product teams. Seen as a risky distraction, few managers volunteered, except for some Individualists and budding Strategists. However, senior management provided sufficient support and feedback to ensure the teams' early success. Soon, the first participants were promoted and leading their own cross-departmental teams. The Achievers in the organization, seeing that others were being promoted, started volunteering for these teams. Gradually, more people within the organization were experiencing shared leadership, mutual testing of one another's assumptions and practices, and individual challenges that contributed to their development as leaders.

Sadly, few companies use teams in this way. Most senior manager teams operate at the Achiever action logic—they prefer unambiguous targets and deadlines, and working with clear strategies, tactics, and plans, often against tight deadlines. They thrive in a climate of adversity ("When the going gets tough, the tough get going") and derive great pleasure from pulling together and delivering. Typically, the team's leaders and several other members will be Achievers, with several Experts and perhaps one or two Individualists or Strategists (who typically feel ignored). Such Achiever teams are often impatient at slowing down to reflect, are apt to dismiss questions about goals and assumptions as "endless philosophizing," and typically respond with hostile humor to creative exercises, calling them "off-the-wall" diversions. These behaviors will ultimately limit an Achiever team's success.

The situation is worse at large, mature companies where senior management teams operate as Experts. Here, vice presidents see themselves as chiefs and their "teams" as an information-reporting formality. Team life is bereft of shared problem-solving, decision-making, or strategy-formulating efforts. Senior teams limited by the Diplomat action logic are even less functional. They are characterized by strong status differences, undiscussable norms, and ritual "court" ceremonies that are carefully stage-managed.

Individualist teams, which are more likely to be found in creative, consulting, and non-profit organizations, are relatively rare and very different from Achiever, Expert, and Diplomat teams. In contrast to Achiever teams, they may be strongly reflective; in fact, excessive time may be spent reviewing goals, assumptions, and work practices. Because individual concerns and input are very important to these teams, rapid decision making may be difficult.

But like individual people, teams can change their style. For instance, we've seen Strategist CEOs help Individualist senior teams balance action and inquiry and so transform into Strategist teams. Another example is an Achiever senior team in a financial services company we worked with that was emerging from two years of harsh cost cutting during a market downturn. To adapt to a changing and growing financial services market, the company needed to become significantly more visionary and innovative and learn how to engage its workforce. To lead this transformation, the team had to start with itself. We worked with it to help team members understand the constraints of the Achiever orientation, which required a number of interventions over time. We began by working to improve the way the team discussed issues and by coaching individual members, including the CEO. As the team evolved, it became apparent that its composition needed to change: Two senior executives, who had initially seemed ideally suited to the group because of their achievements, had to be replaced when it became clear that they were unwilling to engage and experiment with the new approach.

During this reorientation, which lasted slightly more than two years, the team became an Individualist group with emergent Strategist capabilities. The CEO, who had profiled at Achiever/Individualist, now profiled as a Strategist, and most other team members showed one developmental move forward. The impact of this was also felt in the team's and organization's ethos: Once functionally divided, the team learned to accept and integrate the diverse opinions of its members. Employee surveys reported increased engagement across the company. Outsiders began seeing the company as ahead of the curve, which meant the organization was better able to attract top talent. In the third year, bottom- and top-line results were well ahead of industry competitors.

• • •

The leader's voyage of development is not an easy one. Some people change little in their lifetimes; some change substantially. Despite the undeniably crucial role of genetics, human nature is not fixed. Those who are willing to work at developing themselves and becoming more self-aware can almost certainly evolve over time into truly transformational leaders. Few may become Alchemists, but many will have the desire and potential to become Individualists and Strategists. Corporations that help their executives and leadership teams examine their action logics can reap rich rewards.

Reprint R0504D
To order, see the next page
or call 800-988-0886 or 617-783-7500
or go to www.hbrreprints.org

Seven Transformations of Leadership

Further Reading

ARTICLES

Moments of Greatness: Entering the Fundamental State of Leadership
by Robert E. Quinn
Harvard Business Review
July 2005
Product no. R0507K

Changing your action logic requires a significant shift in your thinking processes. In this article, Quinn describes another strategy for changing your thinking process in order to strengthen your leadership skills. This strategy entails asking yourself a series of questions to generate insights into the changes you must make to become a more effective leader. The questions: 1) **"Am I results-centered?"** Have you articulated the results you want to achieve? 2) **"Am I internally directed?"** Are you willing to challenge others' expectations in order to act consistently with your own values? 3) **"Am I other-focused?"** Have you put your organization's needs above your own? 4) **"Am I externally open?"** Do you recognize signals suggesting the need for personal change?

What Makes a Leader?
by Daniel Goleman
Harvard Business Review
February 2000
Product no. R0401H

Upgrading your action logic—whether it's from Expert to Achiever, from Achiever to Individualist, or from Individualist to Strategist or Alchemist—requires **emotional intelligence**, a powerful blend of self-management and relational skills. Goleman defines the five components of emotional intelligence. **Self-management skills** include *self-awareness* (knowledge of your weaknesses and willingness to discuss them), *self-regulation* (the ability to control your impulses and channel them for good), and *motivation* (a passion for achievement for its own sake). **Relational skills** include *empathy* (the capacity to take others' feelings into account while making decisions) and *social skill* (the ability to build rapport with others, win their cooperation, and move them in the direction you desire). To boost your emotional intelligence, commit to making the changes necessary to becoming an effective leader, ask colleagues for feedback on your leadership, and practice the five skills.

Harvard Business Review

www.hbrreprints.org

*Wise executives tailor their
approach to fit the complexity
of the circumstances they face.*

A Leader's Framework
for Decision Making

by David J. Snowden and Mary E. Boone

Wise executives tailor their approach to fit the complexity of the circumstances they face.

A Leader's Framework for Decision Making

by David J. Snowden and Mary E. Boone

In January 1993, a gunman murdered seven people in a fast-food restaurant in Palatine, a suburb of Chicago. In his dual roles as an administrative executive and spokesperson for the police department, Deputy Chief Walter Gasior suddenly had to cope with several different situations at once. He had to deal with the grieving families and a frightened community, help direct the operations of an extremely busy police department, and take questions from the media, which inundated the town with reporters and film crews. "There would literally be four people coming at me with logistics and media issues all at once," he recalls. "And in the midst of all this, we still had a department that had to keep running on a routine basis."

Though Gasior was ultimately successful in juggling multiple demands, not all leaders achieve the desired results when they face situations that require a variety of decisions and responses. All too often, managers rely on common leadership approaches that work well in one set of circumstances but fall short in others. Why do these approaches fail even when logic indicates they should prevail? The answer lies in a fundamental assumption of organizational theory and practice: that a certain level of predictability and order exists in the world. This assumption, grounded in the Newtonian science that underlies scientific management, encourages simplifications that are useful in ordered circumstances. Circumstances change, however, and as they become more complex, the simplifications can fail. Good leadership is not a one-size-fits-all proposition.

We believe the time has come to broaden the traditional approach to leadership and decision making and form a new perspective based on complexity science. (For more on this, see the sidebar "Understanding Complexity.") Over the past ten years, we have applied the principles of that science to governments and a broad range of industries. Working with other contributors, we developed the Cynefin framework, which allows executives to see things from new viewpoints, assimilate complex concepts, and address real-world problems and opportunities. (*Cynefin*, pronounced ku-*nev*-in, is a Welsh word that signifies the multiple factors in our environment and our experience that influence us in ways we can never understand.) Using this approach, leaders learn to define the framework with examples from their own organization's history and scenarios of its possible future. This enhances communication and helps executives rapidly understand the context in which they are operating.

The U.S. Defense Advanced Research Projects Agency has applied the framework to counterterrorism, and it is currently a key component of Singapore's Risk Assessment and Horizon Scanning program. Over time, the framework has evolved through hundreds of applications, from helping a pharmaceutical company develop a new product strategy to assisting a Canadian provincial government in its efforts to engage employees in policy making.

The framework sorts the issues facing leaders into five contexts defined by the nature of the relationship between cause and effect. Four of these—simple, complicated, complex, and chaotic—require leaders to diagnose situations and to act in contextually appropriate ways. The fifth—disorder—applies when it is unclear which of the other four contexts is predominant.

Using the Cynefin framework can help executives sense which context they are in so that they can not only make better decisions but also avoid the problems that arise when their preferred management style causes them to make mistakes. In this article, we focus on the first four contexts, offering examples and suggestions about how to lead and make appropriate decisions in each of them. Since the complex domain is much more prevalent in the business world than most leaders realize—and requires different, often counterintuitive, responses—we concentrate particularly on that context. Leaders who understand that the world is often irrational and unpredictable will find the Cynefin framework particularly useful.

Simple Contexts: The Domain of Best Practice

Simple contexts are characterized by stability and clear cause-and-effect relationships that are easily discernible by everyone. Often, the right answer is self-evident and undisputed. In this realm of "known knowns," decisions are unquestioned because all parties share an understanding. Areas that are little subject to change, such as problems with order processing and fulfillment, usually belong here.

Simple contexts, properly assessed, require straightforward management and monitoring. Here, leaders *sense, categorize*, and *respond*. That is, they assess the facts of the situation, categorize them, and then base their response on established practice. Heavily process-oriented situations, such as loan payment processing, are often simple contexts. If something goes awry, an employee can usually identify the problem (when, say, a borrower pays less than is required), categorize it (review the loan documents to see how partial payments must be processed), and respond appropriately (either not accept the payment or apply the funds according to the terms of the note). Since both managers and employees have access to the information necessary for dealing with the situation in this domain, a command-and-control style for setting parameters works best. Directives are straightforward, decisions can be easily delegated, and functions are automated. Adhering to best practices or process reengineering makes sense. Exhaustive communication among managers and employees is not usually required because disagreement about what needs to be done is rare.

Nevertheless, problems can arise in simple contexts. First, issues may be incorrectly classified within this domain because they have been oversimplified. Leaders who constantly ask for condensed information, regardless of the complexity of the situation, particularly run this risk.

Second, leaders are susceptible to *entrained thinking*, a conditioned response that occurs when people are blinded to new ways of thinking by the perspectives they acquired through past experience, training, and success.

Third, when things appear to be going smoothly, leaders often become complacent. If the context changes at that point, a leader is likely to miss what is happening and react too late. In the exhibit "The Cynefin Framework," the simple domain lies adjacent to the chaotic—and for good reason. The most frequent collapses into chaos occur because

David J. Snowden (snowded@mac.com) is the founder and chief scientific officer of Cognitive Edge, an international research network. He is based primarily in Lockeridge, England. **Mary E. Boone** (mary@maryboone.com) is the president of Boone Associates, a consulting firm in Essex, Connecticut, and the author of numerous books and articles, including *Managing Interactively* (McGraw-Hill, 2001).

success has bred complacency. This shift can bring about catastrophic failure—think of the many previously dominant technologies that were suddenly disrupted by more dynamic alternatives.

Leaders need to avoid micromanaging and stay connected to what is happening in order to spot a change in context. By and large, line workers in a simple situation are more than capable of independently handling any issues that may arise. Indeed, those with years of experience also have deep insight into how the work should be done. Leaders should create a communication channel—an anonymous one, if necessary—that allows dissenters to provide early warnings about complacency.

Finally, it's important to remember that best practice is, by definition, past practice. Using best practices is common, and often appropriate, in simple contexts. Difficulties arise, however, if staff members are discouraged from bucking the process even when it's not working anymore. Since hindsight no longer leads to foresight after a shift in context, a corresponding change in management style may be called for.

Complicated Contexts: The Domain of Experts

Complicated contexts, unlike simple ones, may contain multiple right answers, and though there is a clear relationship between cause and effect, not everyone can see it. This is the realm of "known unknowns." While leaders in a simple context must sense, categorize, and respond to a situation, those in a complicated context must sense, *analyze*, and respond. This approach is not easy and often requires expertise: A motorist may know that something is wrong with his car because the engine is knocking, but he has to take it to a mechanic to diagnose the problem.

Because the complicated context calls for investigating several options—many of which may be excellent—good practice, as opposed to best practice, is more appropriate. For example, the customary approach to engineering a

---

Understanding Complexity

Complexity is more a way of thinking about the world than a new way of working with mathematical models. Over a century ago, Frederick Winslow Taylor, the father of scientific management, revolutionized leadership. Today, advances in complexity science, combined with knowledge from the cognitive sciences, are transforming the field once again. Complexity is poised to help current and future leaders make sense of advanced technology, globalization, intricate markets, cultural change, and much more. In short, the science of complexity can help all of us address the challenges and opportunities we face in a new epoch of human history.

A complex system has the following characteristics:

- It involves large numbers of interacting elements.
- The interactions are nonlinear, and minor changes can produce disproportionately major consequences.
- The system is dynamic, the whole is greater than the sum of its parts, and solutions can't be imposed; rather, they arise from the circumstances. This is

frequently referred to as *emergence*.
- The system has a history, and the past is integrated with the present; the elements evolve with one another and with the environment; and evolution is irreversible.
- Though a complex system may, in retrospect, appear to be ordered and predictable, hindsight does not lead to foresight because the external conditions and systems constantly change.
- Unlike in ordered systems (where the system constrains the agents), or chaotic systems (where there are no constraints), in a complex system the agents and the system constrain one another, especially over time. This means that we cannot forecast or predict what will happen.

One of the early theories of complexity is that complex phenomena arise from simple rules. Consider the rules for the flocking behavior of birds: Fly to the center of the flock, match speed, and avoid collision. This simple-rule theory was applied to industrial modeling and production early on, and it promised much; but it did not deliver in

isolation. More recently, some thinkers and practitioners have started to argue that human complex systems are very different from those in nature and cannot be modeled in the same ways because of human unpredictability and intellect. Consider the following ways in which humans are distinct from other animals:

- They have multiple identities and can fluidly switch between them without conscious thought. (For example, a person can be a respected member of the community as well as a terrorist.)
- They make decisions based on past patterns of success and failure, rather than on logical, definable rules.
- They can, in certain circumstances, purposefully change the systems in which they operate to equilibrium states (think of a Six Sigma project) in order to create predictable outcomes.

Leaders who want to apply the principles of complexity science to their organizations will need to think and act differently than they have in the past. This may not be easy, but it is essential in complex contexts.

new cell phone might emphasize feature A over feature B, but an alternative plan—emphasizing feature C—might be equally valuable.

Another example is the search for oil or mineral deposits. The effort usually requires a team of experts, more than one place will potentially produce results, and the location of the right spots for drilling or mining involves complicated analysis and understanding of consequences at multiple levels.

Entrained thinking is a danger in complicated contexts, too, but it is the experts (rather than the leaders) who are prone to it, and they tend to dominate the domain. When this problem occurs, innovative suggestions by nonexperts may be overlooked or dismissed, resulting in lost opportunities. The experts have, after all, invested in building their knowledge, and they are unlikely to tolerate controversial ideas. If the context has shifted, however, the leader may need access to those maverick concepts. To get around this issue, a leader must listen to the experts while simultaneously welcoming novel thoughts and solutions from others. Executives at one shoe manufacturer did this by opening up the brainstorming process for new shoe styles to the entire company. As a result, a security guard submitted a design for a shoe that became one of their best sellers.

Another potential obstacle is "analysis paralysis," where a group of experts hits a stalemate, unable to agree on any answers because of each individual's entrained thinking—or ego.

Working in unfamiliar environments can help leaders and experts approach decision making more creatively. For instance, we put retail marketing professionals in several military research environments for two weeks. The settings were unfamiliar and challenging, but they shared a primary similarity with the retail environment: In both cases, the marketers had to work with large volumes of data from which it was critical to identify small trends or weak signals. They discovered that there was little difference between, say, handling outgoing disaffected customers and anticipating incoming ballistic missiles. The exercise helped the marketing group learn how to detect a potential loss of loyalty and take action before a valued customer switched to a competitor. By improving their strategy, the marketers were able to retain far more high-volume business.

Games, too, can encourage novel thinking. We created a game played on a fictional planet that was based on the culture of a real client organization. When the executives "landed" on the alien planet, they were asked to address problems and opportunities facing the inhabitants. The issues they encountered were disguised but designed to mirror real situations, many of which were controversial or sensitive. Because the environment seemed so foreign and remote, however, the players found it much easier to come up with fresh ideas than they otherwise might have done. Playing a metaphorical game increases managers' willingness to experiment, allows them to resolve issues or problems more easily

The Cynefin Framework

The Cynefin framework helps leaders determine the prevailing operative context so that they can make appropriate choices. Each domain requires different actions. *Simple* and *complicated* contexts assume an ordered universe, where cause-and-effect relationships are perceptible, and right answers can be determined based on the facts. *Complex* and *chaotic* contexts are unordered—there is no immediately apparent relationship between cause and effect, and the way forward is determined based on emerging patterns. The ordered world is the world of fact-based management; the unordered world represents pattern-based management.

The very nature of the fifth context—*disorder*—makes it particularly difficult to recognize when one is in it. Here, multiple perspectives jostle for prominence, factional leaders argue with one another, and cacophony rules. The way out of this realm is to break down the situation into constituent parts and assign each to one of the other four realms. Leaders can then make decisions and intervene in contextually appropriate ways.

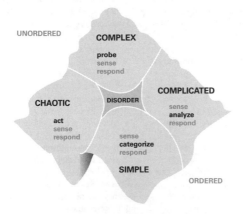

Based on a graphic by Debera Johnson

and creatively, and broadens the range of options in their decision-making processes. The goal of such games is to get as many perspectives as possible to promote unfettered analysis.

Reaching decisions in the complicated domain can often take a lot of time, and there is always a trade-off between finding the right answer and simply making a decision. When the right answer is elusive, however, and you must base your decision on incomplete data, your situation is probably complex rather than complicated.

Complex Contexts: The Domain of Emergence

In a complicated context, at least one right answer exists. In a complex context, however, right answers can't be ferreted out. It's like the difference between, say, a Ferrari and the Brazilian rainforest. Ferraris are complicated machines, but an expert mechanic can take one apart and reassemble it without changing a thing. The car is static, and the whole is the sum of its parts. The rainforest, on the other hand, is in constant flux—a species becomes extinct, weather patterns change, an agricultural project reroutes a water source—and the whole is far more than the sum of its parts. This is the realm of "unknown unknowns," and it is the domain to which much of contemporary business has shifted.

Most situations and decisions in organizations are complex because some major change—a bad quarter, a shift in management, a merger or acquisition—introduces unpredictability and flux. In this domain, we can understand why things happen only in retrospect. Instructive patterns, however, can emerge if the leader conducts experiments that are safe to fail. That is why, instead of attempting to impose a course of action, leaders must patiently allow the path forward to reveal itself. They need to probe first, then sense, and then respond.

There is a scene in the film *Apollo 13* when the astronauts encounter a crisis ("Houston, we have a problem") that moves the situation into a complex domain. A group of experts is put in a room with a mishmash of materials—bits of plastic and odds and ends that mirror the resources available to the astronauts in flight. Leaders tell the team: This is what you have; find a solution or the astronauts will die. None of those experts knew a priori what would work. Instead, they had to let a solution emerge from the materials at hand. And they succeeded. (Conditions of scarcity often produce more creative results than conditions of abundance.)

Another example comes from YouTube. The founders could not possibly have predicted all the applications for streaming video technology that now exist. Once people started using YouTube creatively, however, the company could support and augment the emerging patterns of use. YouTube has become a popular platform for expressing political views, for example. The company built on this pattern by sponsoring a debate for presidential hopefuls with video feeds from the site.

As in the other contexts, leaders face several challenges in the complex domain. Of primary concern is the temptation to fall back into traditional command-and-control management styles—to demand fail-safe business plans with defined outcomes. Leaders who don't recognize that a complex domain requires a more experimental mode of management may become impatient when they don't seem to be achieving the results they were aiming for. They may also find it difficult to tolerate failure, which is an essential aspect of experimental understanding. If they try to overcontrol the organization, they will preempt the opportunity for informative patterns to emerge. Leaders who try to impose order in a complex context will fail, but those who set the stage, step back a bit, allow patterns to emerge, and determine which ones are desirable will succeed. (See the sidebar "Tools for Managing in a Complex Context.") They will discern many opportunities for innovation, creativity, and new business models.

Chaotic Contexts: The Domain of Rapid Response

In a chaotic context, searching for right answers would be pointless: The relationships between cause and effect are impossible to determine because they shift constantly and no manageable patterns exist—only turbulence. This is the realm of unknowables. The events of September 11, 2001, fall into this category.

In the chaotic domain, a leader's immediate job is not to discover patterns but to stanch the bleeding. A leader must first *act* to establish order, then sense where stability is present and from where it is absent, and then respond by working to transform the situation from chaos to complexity, where the identification of emerging patterns can both help prevent future crises and discern new opportunities. Communication of the most direct top-down or broadcast kind is imperative; there's simply no time to ask for input.

Unfortunately, most leadership "recipes" arise from examples of good crisis management. This is a mistake, and not only because chaotic situations are mercifully rare. Though the events of September 11 were not immediately comprehensible, the crisis demanded decisive action. New York's mayor at the time, Rudy Giuliani, demonstrated exceptional effectiveness under chaotic conditions by issuing directives and taking action to re-establish order. However, in his role as mayor—certainly one of the most complex jobs in the world—he was widely criticized for the same top-down leadership style that proved so enormously effective during the catastrophe. He was also criticized afterward for suggesting that elections be postponed so he could maintain order and stability. Indeed, a specific danger for leaders following a crisis is that some of them become less successful when the context shifts because they are not able to switch styles to match it.

Moreover, leaders who are highly successful in chaotic contexts can develop an overinflated self-image, becoming legends in their own minds. When they generate cultlike adoration, leading actually becomes harder for them because a circle of admiring supporters cuts them off from accurate information.

Tools for Managing in a Complex Context

Given the ambiguities of the complex domain, how can leaders lead effectively?

- **Open up the discussion.** Complex contexts require more interactive communication than any of the other domains. Large group methods (LGMs), for instance, are efficient approaches to initiating democratic, interactive, multidirectional discussion sessions. Here, people generate innovative ideas that help leaders with development and execution of complex decisions and strategies. For example, "positive deviance" is a type of LGM that allows people to discuss solutions that are already working within the organization itself, rather than looking to outside best practices for clues about how to proceed. The Plexus Institute used this approach to address the complex problem of hospital-acquired infections, resulting in behavior change that lowered the incidence by as much as 50%.
- **Set barriers.** Barriers limit or delineate behavior. Once the barriers are set, the system can self-regulate within those boundaries. The founders of eBay, for example, created barriers by establishing a simple set of rules. Among them are pay on time, deliver merchandise quickly, and provide full disclosure on the condition of the merchandise. Participants police themselves by rating one another on the quality of their behavior.
- **Stimulate attractors.** Attractors are phenomena that arise when small stimuli and probes (whether from leaders or others) resonate with people. As attractors gain momentum, they provide structure and coherence. EBay again provides an illustrative example. In 1995, founder Pierre Omidyar launched an offering called Auction Web on his personal website. His probe, the first item for sale, quickly morphed into eBay, a remarkable attractor for people who want to buy and sell things. Today, sellers on eBay continue to provide experimental probes that create attractors of various types. One such probe, selling a car on the site, resonated with buyers, and soon automobile sales became a popular attractor.
- **Encourage dissent and diversity.** Dissent and formal debate are valuable communication assets in complex contexts because they encourage the emergence of well-forged patterns and ideas. A "ritual dissent" approach, for instance, puts parallel teams to work on the same problem in a large group meeting environment. Each team appoints a spokesperson who moves from that team's table to another team's table. The spokesperson presents the first group's conclusions while the second group listens in silence. The spokesperson then turns around to face away from the second team, which rips into the presentation, no holds barred, while the spokesperson listens quietly. Each team's spokesperson visits other tables in turn; by the end of the session, all the ideas have been well dissected and honed. Taking turns listening in silence helps everyone understand the value of listening carefully, speaking openly, and not taking criticism personally.
- **Manage starting conditions and monitor for emergence.** Because outcomes are unpredictable in a complex context, leaders need to focus on creating an environment from which good things can emerge, rather than trying to bring about predetermined results and possibly missing opportunities that arise unexpectedly. Many years ago, for instance, 3M instituted a rule allowing its researchers to spend 15% of their time on any project that interested them. One result was a runaway success: the Post-it Note.

Decisions in Multiple Contexts: A Leader's Guide

Effective leaders learn to shift their decision-making styles to match changing business environments. Simple, complicated, complex, and chaotic contexts each call for different managerial responses. By correctly identifying the governing context, staying aware of danger signals, and avoiding inappropriate reactions, managers can lead effectively in a variety of situations.

	THE CONTEXT'S CHARACTERISTICS	THE LEADER'S JOB	DANGER SIGNALS	RESPONSE TO DANGER SIGNALS
SIMPLE	Repeating patterns and consistent events Clear cause-and-effect relationships evident to everyone; right answer exists Known knowns Fact-based management	Sense, categorize, respond Ensure that proper processes are in place Delegate Use best practices Communicate in clear, direct ways Understand that extensive interactive communication may not be necessary	Complacency and comfort Desire to make complex problems simple Entrained thinking No challenge of received wisdom Overreliance on best practice if context shifts	Create communication channels to challenge orthodoxy Stay connected without micromanaging Don't assume things are simple Recognize both the value and the limitations of best practice
COMPLICATED	Expert diagnosis required Cause-and-effect relationships discoverable but not immediately apparent to everyone; more than one right answer possible Known unknowns Fact-based management	Sense, analyze, respond Create panels of experts Listen to conflicting advice	Experts overconfident in their own solutions or in the efficacy of past solutions Analysis paralysis Expert panels Viewpoints of nonexperts excluded	Encourage external and internal stakeholders to challenge expert opinions to combat entrained thinking Use experiments and games to force people to think outside the familiar
COMPLEX	Flux and unpredictability No right answers; emergent instructive patterns Unknown unknowns Many competing ideas A need for creative and innovative approaches Pattern-based leadership	Probe, sense, respond Create environments and experiments that allow patterns to emerge Increase levels of interaction and communication Use methods that can help generate ideas: Open up discussion (as through large group methods); set barriers; stimulate attractors; encourage dissent and diversity; and manage starting conditions and monitor for emergence	Temptation to fall back into habitual, command-and-control mode Temptation to look for facts rather than allowing patterns to emerge Desire for accelerated resolution of problems or exploitation of opportunities	Be patient and allow time for reflection Use approaches that encourage interaction so patterns can emerge
CHAOTIC	High turbulence No clear cause-and-effect relationships, so no point in looking for right answers Unknowables Many decisions to make and no time to think High tension Pattern-based leadership	Act, sense, respond Look for what works instead of seeking right answers Take immediate action to reestablish order (command and control) Provide clear, direct communication	Applying a command-and-control approach longer than needed "Cult of the leader" Missed opportunity for innovation Chaos unabated	Set up mechanisms (such as parallel teams) to take advantage of opportunities afforded by a chaotic environment Encourage advisers to challenge your point of view once the crisis has abated Work to shift the context from chaotic to complex

Yet the chaotic domain is nearly always the best place for leaders to impel innovation. People are more open to novelty and directive leadership in these situations than they would be in other contexts. One excellent technique is to manage chaos and innovation in parallel: The minute you encounter a crisis, appoint a reliable manager or crisis management team to resolve the issue. At the same time, pick out a separate team and focus its members on the opportunities for doing things differently. If you wait until the crisis is over, the chance will be gone.

Leadership Across Contexts

Good leadership requires openness to change on an individual level. Truly adept leaders will know not only how to identify the context they're working in at any given time but also how to change their behavior and their decisions to match that context. They also prepare their organization to understand the different contexts and the conditions for transition between them. Many leaders lead effectively—though usually in only one or two domains (not in all of them) and few, if any, prepare their organizations for diverse contexts.

During the Palatine murders of 1993, Deputy Chief Gasior faced four contexts at once. He had to take immediate action via the media to stem the tide of initial panic by keeping the community informed (chaotic); he had to help keep the department running routinely and according to established procedure (simple); he had to call in experts (complicated); and he had to continue to calm the community in the days and weeks following the crime (complex). That last situation proved the most challenging. Parents were afraid to let their children go to school, and employees were concerned about safety in their workplaces. Had Gasior misread the context as simple, he might just have said, "Carry on," which would have done nothing to reassure the community. Had he misread it as complicated, he might have called in experts to say it was safe—risking a loss of credibility and trust. Instead, Gasior set up a forum for business owners, high school students, teachers, and parents to share concerns and hear the facts. It was the right approach for a complex context: He allowed solutions to emerge from the community itself rather than trying to impose them.

• • •

Business schools and organizations equip leaders to operate in ordered domains (simple and complicated), but most leaders usually must rely on their natural capabilities when operating in unordered contexts (complex and chaotic). In the face of greater complexity today, however, intuition, intellect, and charisma are no longer enough. Leaders need tools and approaches to guide their firms through less familiar waters.

In the complex environment of the current business world, leaders often will be called upon to act against their instincts. They will need to know when to share power and when to wield it alone, when to look to the wisdom of the group and when to take their own counsel. A deep understanding of context, the ability to embrace complexity and paradox, and a willingness to flexibly change leadership style will be required for leaders who want to make things happen in a time of increasing uncertainty.

Reprint R0711C
To order, see the next page
or call 800-988-0886 or 617-783-7500
or go to www.hbrreprints.org

Further Reading

We look for lessons in the actions of great leaders. We should instead be examining what goes on in their heads— particularly the way they creatively build on the tensions among conflicting ideas.

How Successful Leaders Think

by Roger Martin

Included with this full-text *Harvard Business Review* article:

Reprint R0706C

How Successful Leaders Think

The Idea in Brief

The secret to becoming a great leader? Don't *act* like one, Martin advises. Instead, *think* like one.

Brilliant leaders excel at **integrative thinking**. They can hold two opposing ideas in their minds at once. Then, rather than settling for choice A or B, they forge an innovative "third way" that contains elements of both but improves on each.

Consider Bob Young, cofounder of Red Hat, the dominant distributor of Linux open-source software. The business model Young created for Red Hat transcended the two prevailing software industry models— winning Red Hat entrée into the lucrative corporate market.

How to become an integrative thinker? Resist the simplicity and certainty that comes with conventional "either-or" thinking. Embrace the messiness and complexity of conflicting options. And emulate great leaders' decision-making approach— looking *beyond* obvious considerations.

Your reward? Instead of making unattractive trade-offs, you generate a wealth of profitable solutions for your business.

The Idea in Practice

What does integrative thinking look like in action? Contrast conventional and integrative thinkers' approaches to the four steps of decision making:

STEP 1: IDENTIFYING KEY FACTORS

Conventional thinkers consider only obviously relevant factors while weighing options. **Integrative thinkers** seek less obvious but potentially more relevant considerations.

▶ Example:

Bob Young disliked the two prevailing software business models: selling operating software but not source code needed to develop software applications (profitable but anathema to open-source advocates) or selling CD-ROMs containing software and source code (aligned with open-source values but not profitable). Seeking a third choice, he considered CIOs' reluctance to buy new technology that would be complicated to maintain. Viewing their reluctance as relevant eventually helped Young see that selling software *service* would be a superior alternative to the existing *product*-based business models.

STEP 2: ANALYZING CAUSALITY

Conventional thinkers consider one-way, linear relationships between factors: more of A produces more of B. **Integrative thinkers** consider multidirectional relationships.

▶ Example:

Young analyzed the complex relationships among pricing, profitability, and distribution channels. He recognized that a product based on freely available components would soon become a commodity. Any electronics retailer could assemble its own Linux product and push it through its well-developed distribution channel—leaving Red Hat stranded. Analysis of these causal relationships yielded a nuanced picture of the industry's future.

STEP 3: ENVISIONING THE DECISION'S OVERALL STRUCTURE

Conventional thinkers break a problem into pieces and work on them separately. **Integrative thinkers** see a problem as a whole— examining how its various aspects affect one another.

▶ Example:

Young held several issues in his head simultaneously, including CIOs' concerns, dynamics of individual and corporate markets for system software, and the evolving economics of the free-software business. Each "piece" could have pushed him toward a separate decision. But by considering the issues as an interrelated whole, Young began to realize only one player would ultimately dominate the corporate market.

STEP 4: ACHIEVING RESOLUTION

Conventional thinkers make either-or choices. **Integrative thinkers** refuse to accept conventional options.

▶ Example:

To pursue market leadership, Young devised an unconventional business model. The model synthesized two seemingly irreconcilable models by combining low product price with profitable service offerings. Red Hat began helping companies manage the software upgrades available almost daily through Linux's open-source platform. It also gave the software away as a free Internet download. Thus, Red Hat acquired the scale and market leadership to attract cautious corporate customers to what became its central offering: service, not software.

We look for lessons in the actions of great leaders. We should instead be examining what goes on in their heads—particularly the way they creatively build on the tensions among conflicting ideas.

How Successful Leaders Think

by Roger Martin

We are drawn to the stories of effective leaders in action. Their decisiveness invigorates us. The events that unfold from their bold moves, often culminating in successful outcomes, make for gripping narratives. Perhaps most important, we turn to accounts of their deeds for lessons that we can apply in our own careers. Books like *Jack: Straight from the Gut* and *Execution: The Discipline of Getting Things Done* are compelling in part because they implicitly promise that we can achieve the success of a Jack Welch or a Larry Bossidy—if only we learn to emulate his actions.

But this focus on *what a leader does* is misplaced. That's because moves that work in one context often make little sense in another, even at the same company or within the experience of a single leader. Recall that Jack Welch, early in his career at General Electric, insisted that each of GE's businesses be number one or number two in market share in its industry; years later he insisted that those same businesses define their markets so that their share was no greater than 10%, thereby forcing managers to look for opportunities beyond the confines of a narrowly conceived market. Trying to learn from what Jack Welch did invites confusion and incoherence, because he pursued—wisely, I might add—diametrically opposed courses at different points in his career and in GE's history.

So where do we look for lessons? A more productive, though more difficult, approach is to focus on *how a leader thinks*—that is, to examine the antecedent of doing, or the ways in which leaders' cognitive processes produce their actions.

I have spent the past 15 years, first as a management consultant and now as the dean of a business school, studying leaders with exemplary records. Over the past six years, I have interviewed more than 50 such leaders, some for as long as eight hours, and found that most of them share a somewhat unusual trait: They have the predisposition and the capacity to hold in their heads two opposing ideas at once. And then, without panicking or simply settling for one alternative or the other, they're able to creatively resolve the tension between those two ideas by generating a new one that contains elements of the others but is superior to both. This process of consideration and synthesis can be termed integrative thinking. It is this discipline—not superior strategy or faultless execution—that is a defining characteristic of most exceptional businesses and the people who run them.

I don't claim that this is a new idea. More than 60 years ago, F. Scott Fitzgerald saw "the ability to hold two opposing ideas in mind at the same time and still retain the ability to function" as the sign of a truly intelligent individual. And certainly not every good leader exhibits this capability, nor is it the sole source of success for those who do. But it is clear to me that integrative thinking tremendously improves people's odds.

This insight is easy to miss, though, since the management conversation in recent years has tilted away from thinking and toward doing (witness the popularity of books like *Execution*). Also, many great integrative thinkers aren't even aware of their particular capability and thus don't consciously exercise it. Take Jack Welch, who is among the executives I have interviewed: He is clearly a consummate integrative thinker—but you'd never know it from reading his books.

Indeed, my aim in this article is to deconstruct and describe a capability that seems to come naturally to many successful leaders. To illustrate the concept, I'll concentrate on an executive I talked with at length: Bob Young, the colorful cofounder and former CEO of Red Hat, the dominant distributor of Linux open-source software. The assumption underlying my examination of his and others' integrative thinking is this: It isn't just an ability you're born with—it's something you can hone.

Opposable Thumb, Opposable Mind

In the mid-1990s, Red Hat faced what seemed like two alternative paths to growth. At the time, the company sold packaged versions of Linux open-source software, mainly to computer geeks, periodically bundling together new versions that included the latest upgrades from countless independent developers. As Red Hat looked to grow beyond its $1 million in annual sales, it could have chosen one of the two basic business models in the software industry.

One was the classic proprietary-software model, employed by big players such as Microsoft, Oracle, and SAP, which sold customers operating software but not the source code. These companies invested heavily in research and development, guarded their intellectual property jealously, charged high prices, and enjoyed wide profit margins because their customers, lacking access to the source code, were essentially locked into purchasing regular upgrades.

The alternative, employed by numerous small companies, including Red Hat itself, was the so-called free-software model, in which suppliers sold CD-ROMs with both the software and the source code. The software products weren't in fact free, but prices were modest—$15 for a packaged version of the Linux operating system versus more than $200 for Microsoft Windows. Suppliers made money each time they assembled a new version from the many free updates by independent developers; but profit margins were narrow and revenue was uncertain. Corporate customers, looking for standardization and predictability, were wary not only of the unfamiliar software but also of its small and idiosyncratic suppliers.

Bob Young—a self-deprecating eccentric in an industry full of eccentrics, who signaled his affiliation with his company by regularly sporting red socks and a red hat—didn't like either of these models. The high-margin proprietary model ran counter to the whole philosophy of Linux and the open-source movement, even if there had been a way to create proprietary versions of the software. "Buying proprietary software is like buying a car with the hood welded shut," Young told me. "If something goes wrong, you can't even try to fix it." But the free-software model meant scraping a slim profit from the packaging and distribution of a freely available commodity in a fringe market, which might have offered reasonable returns in the short term but wasn't likely to deliver sustained profitable growth.

Young likes to say that he's not "one of the smart guys" in the industry, that he's a salesman in a world of technical geniuses. Nonetheless, he managed to synthesize two seemingly irreconcilable business models, placing Red Hat on a path to tremendous success. His response to his strategic dilemma was to combine the free-software model's low product price with the proprietary model's profitable

Roger Martin (martin@rotman .utoronto.ca) is the dean of the Rotman School of Management at the University of Toronto and the author of *The Opposable Mind: How Successful Leaders Win Through Integrative Thinking*, forthcoming from Harvard Business School Press in the fall of 2007.

service component, in the process creating something new: a corporate market for the Linux operating system. As is often the case with integrative thinking, Young included some twists on both models that made the synthesis work.

Although inspired by the proprietary model, Red Hat's service offering was quite different. "If you ran into a bug that caused your systems to crash," Young said of the service you'd buy from the big proprietary shops, "you would call up the manufacturer and say, 'My systems are crashing.' And he'd say, 'Oh, dear,' while he really meant, 'Oh, good.' He'd send an engineer over at several hundred dollars an hour to fix his software, which was broken when he delivered it to you, and he'd call that customer service." Red Hat, by contrast, helped companies manage the upgrades and improvements available almost daily through Linux's open-source platform.

Young also made a crucial change to what had been the somewhat misleadingly dubbed free-software model: He actually gave the software away, repackaging it as a free download on the Internet rather than as an inexpensive but cumbersome CD-ROM. This allowed Red Hat to break away from the multitude of small Linux packagers by acquiring the scale and market leadership to generate faith among cautious corporate customers in what would become Red Hat's central offering—service, not software.

In 1999, Red Hat went public, and Young became a billionaire on the first day of trading. By 2000, Linux had captured 25% of the server operating system market, and Red Hat held more than 50% of the global market for Linux systems. Unlike the vast majority of dot-com era start-ups, Red Hat has continued to grow.

What enabled Young to resolve the apparent choice between two unattractive models? It was his use of an innate but underdeveloped human characteristic, something we might call—in a metaphor that echoes another human trait—the opposable mind.

Human beings are distinguished from nearly every other creature by a physical feature: the opposable thumb. Thanks to the tension that we can create by opposing the thumb and fingers, we can do marvelous things—write, thread a needle, guide a catheter through an artery. Although evolution provided human beings with this potential advan-

tage, it would have gone to waste if our species had not exercised it in ever more sophisticated ways. When we engage in something like writing, we train the muscles involved and the brain that controls them. Without exploring the possibilities of opposition, we wouldn't have developed either its physical properties or the cognition that accompanies and animates it.

Analogously, we were born with opposable minds, which allow us to hold two conflicting ideas in constructive, almost dialectic tension. We can use that tension to think our way toward new, superior ideas. Were we able to hold only one thought or idea in our heads at a time, we wouldn't have access to the insights that the opposable mind can produce.

Unfortunately, because people don't exercise this capability much, great integrative thinkers are fairly rare. Why is this potentially powerful but generally latent tool used so infrequently and to less than full advantage? Because putting it to work makes us anxious. Most of us avoid complexity and ambiguity and seek out the comfort of simplicity and clarity. To cope with the dizzying complexity of the world around us, we simplify where we can. We crave the certainty of choosing between well-defined alternatives and the closure that comes when a decision has been made.

For those reasons, we often don't know what to do with fundamentally opposing and seemingly incommensurable models. Our first impulse is usually to determine which of the two models is "right" and, by the process of elimination, which is "wrong." We may even take sides and try to prove that our chosen model is better than the other one. But in rejecting one model out of hand, we miss out on all the value that we could have realized by considering the opposing two at the same time and finding in the tension clues to a superior model. By forcing a choice between the two, we disengage the opposable mind before it can seek a creative resolution.

This nearly universal personal trait is writ large in most organizations. When a colleague admonishes us to "quit complicating the issue," it's not just an impatient reminder to get on with the damn job—it's also a plea to keep complexity at a comfortable level.

To take advantage of our opposable minds, we must resist our natural leaning toward simplicity and certainty. Bob Young recognized from the beginning that he wasn't bound to

We often don't know what to do with fundamentally opposing models. Our first impulse is usually to determine which is "right" and, by the process of elimination, which is "wrong."

choose one of the two prevailing software business models. He saw the unpleasant trade-offs he'd have to make if he chose between the two as a signal to rethink the problem from the ground up. And he didn't rest until he found a new model that grew out of the tension between them.

Basically, Young refused to settle for an "either-or" choice. That phrase has come up time and again in my interviews with successful leaders. When asked whether he thought strategy or execution was more important, Jack Welch responded: "I don't think it's an 'either-or.'" Similarly, Procter & Gamble CEO A.G. Lafley—when asked how he came up with a turnaround plan that drew on both cost cutting and investment in innovation—said: "We weren't going to win if it were an 'or.' Everybody can do 'or.'"

The Four Stages of Decision Making
So what does the process of integrative thinking look like? How do integrative thinkers consider their options in a way that leads to new possibilities and not merely back to the same inadequate alternatives? They work through four related but distinct stages. The steps themselves aren't particular to integrative thinking: Everyone goes through them while thinking through a decision. What's distinc-

tive about integrative thinkers is how they approach the steps. (See the exhibit "Conventional Versus Integrative Thinking.")

Determining salience. The first step is figuring out which factors to take into account. The conventional approach is to discard as many as possible—or not even to consider some of them in the first place. In order to reduce our exposure to uncomfortable complexity, we filter out salient features when considering an issue.

We also do this because of how most organizations are structured. Each functional specialty has its own narrow view of what merits consideration. Finance departments haven't traditionally regarded emotional factors as salient; similarly, departments concerned with organizational behavior have often ignored quantitative questions. Managers pressure employees to limit their view of what's salient to match the department's doctrine, leaving people with only a subset of the factors to which they might otherwise have productively paid attention.

When our decisions turn out badly, we often recognize after the fact that we've failed to consider factors that are significant to those outside the immediate reach of our jobs or functional specialties. We say to ourselves, "I should have thought about how the employees in our European operation would have inter-

Conventional Versus Integrative Thinking

When responding to problems or challenges, leaders work through four steps. Those who are conventional thinkers seek simplicity along the way and are often forced to make unattractive trade-offs. By contrast, integrative thinkers welcome complexity—even if it means repeating one or more of the steps—and this allows them to craft innovative solutions.

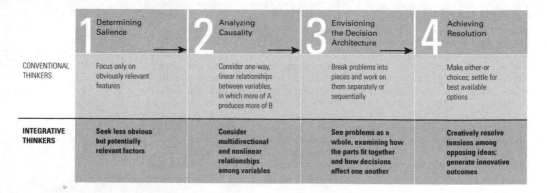

	1 Determining Salience	2 Analyzing Causality	3 Envisioning the Decision Architecture	4 Achieving Resolution
CONVENTIONAL THINKERS	Focus only on obviously relevant features	Consider one-way, linear relationships between variables, in which more of A produces more of B	Break problems into pieces and work on them separately or sequentially	Make either-or choices; settle for best available options
INTEGRATIVE THINKERS	**Seek less obvious but potentially relevant factors**	**Consider multidirectional and nonlinear relationships among variables**	**See problems as a whole, examining how the parts fit together and how decisions affect one another**	**Creatively resolve tensions among opposing ideas; generate innovative outcomes**

preted the wording of that memo" or "I should have thought about the state's road-repair program before choosing a site for our new distribution center." The integrative thinker, by contrast, actively seeks less obvious but potentially relevant factors. Of course, more salient features make for a messier problem, but integrative thinkers don't mind the mess. In fact, they embrace it, because it assures them that they haven't dismissed anything that may illuminate the problem as a whole. They welcome complexity, because that's where the best answers come from. They are confident that they'll find their way through it and emerge on the other side with a clear resolution.

In his thinking about a new business model for Red Hat, Bob Young added into his calculations something ignored both by software companies generally and by Linux suppliers in particular: the day-to-day concerns of corporate CIOs and their systems administrators. Doing this allowed him to envision an innovative model that tapped into an entirely new market for Linux-based products and services.

As a whole, the software industry disdains CIOs' reluctance to buy the newest and best technology, attributing it to timidity or strict adherence to the "you'll never get fired for buying IBM" mantra. Young not only empathized with the CIOs but found their caution understandable. "It's *not* FUD—fear, uncertainty, and doubt," he said. "It's sensible."

Linux software was an entirely new product for corporate buyers, one that didn't follow any familiar rules. It was free. No one supplier controlled it. Thousands of versions were out there, and each one changed nearly every day. From the CIOs' perspective, that Linux was cheaper and better than Windows-based products—the basic sales message delivered by Red Hat's rivals—played a relatively small part in the calculation. The CIOs were thinking about whether their investment would be in a stable and consistent platform that would work across their organizations and whether their suppliers would still be around in ten or 15 years. Systems administrators worried that the complexity of Linux—with its random and almost daily upgrades—would create a management nightmare, since different teams of people throughout the company would have to maintain the software packages.

Viewing these concerns as salient helped lead Young to conclude that, in the case of Linux, service was a bigger selling point than product and that a vendor's long-term credibility was crucial.

Analyzing causality. In the second step of decision making, you analyze how the numerous salient factors relate to one another. Conventional thinkers tend to take the same narrow view of causality that they do of salience. The simplest type of all is a straight-line causal relationship. It's no accident that linear regression is the business world's preferred tool for establishing relationships between variables. Other tools are available, of course, but most managers shun them because they're harder to use. How many times has a superior scolded you for making a problem more complicated than it needs to be? You protest that you're not trying to complicate anything; you just want to see the problem as it really is. Your boss tells you to stick to your job, and a potentially complex relationship becomes a linear one in which more of A produces more of B.

When we make bad decisions, sometimes it is because we got the causal links between salient features wrong. We may have been right about the direction of a relationship but wrong about the magnitude: "I thought that our costs would decrease much faster than they actually did as our scale grew." Or we may have gotten the direction of a relationship wrong: "I thought that our capacity to serve clients would increase when we hired a new batch of consultants, but it actually shrank, because the experienced consultants had to spend a huge amount of their time training the new ones and fixing their rookie mistakes."

The integrative thinker isn't afraid to question the validity of apparently obvious links or to consider multidirectional and nonlinear relationships. So, for example, rather than simply thinking, "That competitor's price-cutting is hurting our bottom line," the integrative thinker may conclude, "Our product introduction really upset our rivals. Now they're cutting prices in response, and our profitability is suffering."

The most interesting causal link that Young identified was the rather subtle one between the free availability of Red Hat software's basic components and the likely—or inevitable, in Young's view—evolution of the industry. The relationships he saw between pricing, profitability, and distribution channel drove his company in a different direction from its

Integrative thinkers don't mind a messy problem. In fact, they welcome complexity, because that's where the best answers come from.

Linux competitors, which saw a perfectly good market for their "free" software. This is what allowed him to create and then lock up the new corporate market.

For example, Young recognized the vulnerability of a product based on freely available components. Whatever you charged for the convenience of getting a Linux operating system bundled together on one CD-ROM, inevitably "someone else would come in and price it lower," he said. "It was a commodity in the truest sense of the word." He also realized that a company that wasn't a current rival—say, a big electronics retailer—could put together a Linux product of its own and then push it through its own well-developed distribution channel, leaving Red Hat and other suppliers out in the cold. "I knew I needed a product I had some control over so I could make CompUSA a customer"—that is, a corporate purchaser of Red Hat's service package—"rather than a competitor" with its own CD-ROM product.

The causal relationships spotted by Young weren't earth-shattering on their own, but putting them together helped Young create a more nuanced picture of the industry's future than his competitors were able to.

Envisioning the decision architecture. With a good handle on the causal relationships between salient features, you're ready to turn to the decision itself. But which decision? Even the simple question of whether to go to a movie tonight involves deciding, at the very least, which movie to see, which theater to go to, and which showing to attend. The order in which you make these decisions will affect the outcome. For example, you may not be able to see your preferred movie if you've already decided you need to be back in time to relieve a babysitter who has plans for later in the evening. When you're trying to invent a new business model, the number of decision-making variables explodes. And with that comes the impulse not only to establish a strict sequence in which issues will be considered but also to dole out pieces of a decision so that various parties—often, different corporate functions—can work on them separately.

What usually happens is that everyone loses sight of the overriding issue, and a mediocre outcome results. Suppose that Bob Young had delegated to different functional heads questions concerning the pricing, enhancement,

and distribution of Red Hat's original software product. Would their individual answers, agglomerated into an overall Red Hat strategy, have produced the spectacularly successful new business model that Young came up with? It doesn't seem all that likely.

Integrative thinkers don't break down a problem into independent pieces and work on them separately or in a certain order. They see the entire architecture of the problem—how the various parts of it fit together, how one decision will affect another. Just as important, they hold all of those pieces suspended in their minds at once. They don't parcel out the elements for others to work on piecemeal or let one element temporarily drop out of sight, only to be taken up again for consideration after everything else has been decided. An architect doesn't ask his subordinates to design a perfect bathroom and a perfect living room and a perfect kitchen, and then hope that the pieces of the house will fit nicely together. A business executive doesn't design a product before considering the costs of manufacturing it.

Young held simultaneously in his head a number of issues: the feelings and the challenges of chief information officers and systems administrators, the dynamics of both the individual and the corporate markets for operating system software, the evolving economics of the free-software business, and the motivations behind the major players in the proprietary-software business. Each factor could have pushed him toward a separate decision on how to address the challenge. But he delayed making decisions and considered the relationships between these issues as he slowly moved toward the creation of a new business model, one based on the belief that dominant market share would be critical to Red Hat's success.

Achieving resolution. All of these stages—determining what is salient, analyzing the causal relationships between the salient factors, examining the architecture of the problem—lead to an outcome. Too often, we accept an unpleasant trade-off with relatively little complaint, since it appears to be the best alternative. That's because by the time we have reached this stage, our desire for simplicity has led us to ignore opportunities in the previous three steps to discover interesting and novel ways around the trade-off. Instead of rebelling against the meager and unattractive alternatives, instead of refusing to settle for the best available bad choice, the conventional thinker shrugs and asks, "What else could we have done?"

"Much else," the integrative thinker says. A leader who embraces holistic rather than segmented thinking can creatively resolve the tensions that launched the decision-making process. The actions associated with the search for such resolution—creating delays, sending teams back to examine things more deeply, generating new options at the 11th hour—can appear irresolute from the outside. Indeed, the integrative thinker may even be dissatisfied with the fresh batch of options he's come up with, in which case he may go back and start over. When a satisfactory outcome does emerge, though, it is inevitably due to the leader's refusal to accept trade-offs and conventional options.

The outcome in the case of Red Hat was completely unconventional—not many companies suddenly decide to give away their products—and ultimately successful. Young's gradual realization that only one player in his industry would have leverage with and support from corporate customers—and that such leverage and support could reap attractive service revenues from totally free software—shaped the dramatically creative decision he made.

The thinking that he intuitively engaged in is very different from the thinking that produces most managerial decisions. But, he said, his experience was hardly unique: "People are often faced with difficult choices—for instance, 'Do I want to be the high-quality, high-cost supplier or the low-quality, low-cost supplier?' We're trained to examine the pros and cons of such alternatives and then pick one of them. But really successful businesspeople look at choices like these and say, 'I don't like either one.'" Using that recurring phrase, he added: "They don't accept that it's an 'either-or.'"

Born and Bred
The consequences of integrative thinking and conventional thinking couldn't be more distinct. Integrative thinking generates options and new solutions. It creates a sense of limitless possibility. Conventional thinking glosses over potential solutions and fosters the illusion that creative solutions don't actually exist. With integrative thinking, aspirations rise over time. With conventional thinking, they wear away with every apparent reinforcement of the les-

son that life is about accepting unattractive trade-offs. Fundamentally, the conventional thinker prefers to accept the world just as it is, whereas the integrative thinker welcomes the challenge of shaping the world for the better.

Given the benefits of integrative thinking, you have to ask, "If I'm not an integrative thinker, can I learn to be one?" In F. Scott Fitzgerald's view, only people with "first-rate intelligence" can continue to function while holding two opposing ideas in their heads. But I refuse to believe that the ability to use our opposable minds is a gift reserved for a small minority of people. I prefer the view suggested by Thomas C. Chamberlin, a nineteenth-century American geologist and former president of the University of Wisconsin. More than 100 years ago, Chamberlin wrote an article in *Science* magazine proposing the idea of "multiple working hypotheses" as an improvement over the most commonly employed scientific method of the time: testing the validity of a single hypothesis through trial and error. Chamberlin argued that his approach would provide more accurate explanations of scientific phenomena by taking into account "the co-ordination of several agencies, which enter into the combined result in varying proportions." While acknowledging the cognitive challenges posed by such an approach, Chamberlin wrote that it "develops a habit of thought analogous to the method itself, which may be designated a habit of parallel or complex thought. Instead of a simple succession of thoughts in linear order…the mind appears to become possessed of the power of simultaneous vision from different standpoints."

Similarly, I believe that integrative thinking is a "habit of thought" that all of us can consciously develop to arrive at solutions that would otherwise not be evident. First, there needs to be greater general awareness of integrative thinking as a concept. Then, over time, we can teach it in our business schools—an endeavor that colleagues and I are currently working on. At some point, integrative thinking will no longer be just a tacit skill (cultivated knowingly or not) in the heads of a select few.

Reprint R0706C
To order, see the next page
or call 800-988-0886 or 617-783-7500
or go to www.hbrreprints.org

How Successful Leaders Think

Further Reading

ARTICLE

The Seasoned Executive's Decision-Making Style
by Kenneth R. Brousseau, Michael J. Driver,
Gary Hourihan, and Rikard Larsson
Harvard Business Review
February 2006
Product no. R0602F

The authors affirm the importance of "integrative thinking" to leadership success. But they also argue that integrative thinking may not always create advantage for lower-level managers. At lower levels, the job is to get widgets out the door (or solve glitches on the spot). Action is at a premium. At higher levels, the job involves making decisions about which widgets or services to offer and how to develop them. To climb the corporate ladder and be effective in new roles, managers must change their decision-making styles. Making decisions like a full-fledged senior executive too soon can hurl an ambitious manager right off the fast track. And it's just as destructive to act like a first-line supervisor after being bumped up to senior management. By understanding the distinguishing characteristics of four different decision-making styles, managers can ensure that they use the right ones during each stage in their career.

Harvard Business Review 🛡

To Order

For *Harvard Business Review* reprints and subscriptions, call 800-988-0886 or 617-783-7500. Go to www.hbrreprints.org

For customized and quantity orders of *Harvard Business Review* article reprints, call 617-783-7626, or e-mail customizations@hbsp.harvard.edu

Harvard Business Review ▪

www.hbrreprints.org

Teams whose members come from different nations and backgrounds place special demands on managers— especially when a feuding team looks to the boss for help with a conflict.

Managing Multicultural Teams

by Jeanne Brett, Kristin Behfar, and Mary C. Kern

Included with this full-text *Harvard Business Review* article:

Managing Multicultural Teams

The Idea in Brief

If your company does business internationally, you're probably leading teams with members from diverse cultural backgrounds. Those differences can present serious obstacles. For example, some members' lack of fluency in the team's dominant language can lead others to underestimate their competence. When such obstacles arise, your team can stalemate.

To get the team moving again, avoid intervening directly, advise Brett, Behfar, and Kern. Though sometimes necessary, your involvement can prevent team members from solving problems themselves—and learning from that process.

Instead, choose one of three indirect interventions. When possible, encourage team members to **adapt** by acknowledging cultural gaps and working around them. If your team isn't able to be open about their differences, consider **structural intervention** (e.g., reassigning members to reduce interpersonal friction). As a last resort, use an **exit** strategy (e.g., removing a member from the team).

There's no one right way to tackle multicultural problems. But understanding four barriers to team success can help you begin evaluating possible responses.

The Idea in Practice

FOUR BARRIERS

The following cultural differences can cause destructive conflicts in a team:

- **Direct versus indirect communication.** Some team members use direct, explicit communication while others are indirect, for example, asking questions instead of pointing out problems with a project. When members see such differences as violations of their culture's communication norms, relationships can suffer.

- **Trouble with accents and fluency.** Members who aren't fluent in the team's dominant language may have difficulty communicating their knowledge. This can prevent the team from using their expertise and create frustration or perceptions of incompetence.

- **Differing attitudes toward hierarchy.** Team members from hierarchical cultures expect to be treated differently according to their status in the organization. Members from egalitarian cultures do not. Failure of some members to honor those expectations can cause humiliation or loss of stature and credibility.

- **Conflicting decision-making norms.** Members vary in how quickly they make decisions and in how much analysis they require beforehand. Someone who prefers making decisions quickly may grow frustrated with those who need more time.

FOUR INTERVENTIONS

Your team's unique circumstances can help you determine how to respond to multicultural conflicts. Consider these options:

Intervention Type	When to Use	Example
Adaptation: working with or around differences	Members are willing to acknowledge cultural differences and figure out how to live with them.	An American engineer working on a team that included Israelis was shocked by their in your face, argumentative style. Once he noticed they confronted each other and not just him—and still worked well together—he realized confrontations weren't personal attacks and accepted their style.
Structural intervention: reorganizing to reduce friction	The team has obvious subgroups, or members cling to negative stereotypes of one another.	An international research team's leader realized that when he led meetings, members "shut down" because they felt intimidated by his executive status. After he hired a consultant to run future meetings, members participated more.
Managerial intervention: making final decisions without team involvement	Rarely; for instance, a new team needs guidance in establishing productive norms.	A software development team's lingua franca was English, but some members spoke with pronounced accents. The manager explained they'd been chosen for their task expertise, not fluency in English. And she directed them to tell customers: "I realize I have an accent. If you don't understand what I'm saying, just stop me and ask questions."
Exit: voluntary or involuntary removal of a team member	Emotions are running high, and too much face has been lost on both sides to salvage the situation.	When two members of a multicultural consulting team couldn't resolve their disagreement over how to approach problems, one member left the firm.

Teams whose members come from different nations and backgrounds place special demands on managers—especially when a feuding team looks to the boss for help with a conflict.

Managing Multicultural Teams

by Jeanne Brett, Kristin Behfar, and Mary C. Kern

When a major international software developer needed to produce a new product quickly, the project manager assembled a team of employees from India and the United States. From the start the team members could not agree on a delivery date for the product. The Americans thought the work could be done in two to three weeks; the Indians predicted it would take two to three months. As time went on, the Indian team members proved reluctant to report setbacks in the production process, which the American team members would find out about only when work was due to be passed to them. Such conflicts, of course, may affect any team, but in this case they arose from cultural differences. As tensions mounted, conflict over delivery dates and feedback became personal, disrupting team members' communication about even mundane issues. The project manager decided he had to intervene—with the result that both the American and the Indian team members came to rely on him for direction regarding minute operational

details that the team should have been able to handle itself. The manager became so bogged down by quotidian issues that the project careened hopelessly off even the most pessimistic schedule—and the team never learned to work together effectively.

Multicultural teams often generate frustrating management dilemmas. Cultural differences can create substantial obstacles to effective teamwork—but these may be subtle and difficult to recognize until significant damage has already been done. As in the case above, which the manager involved told us about, managers may create more problems than they resolve by intervening. The challenge in managing multicultural teams effectively is to recognize underlying cultural causes of conflict, and to intervene in ways that both get the team back on track and empower its members to deal with future challenges themselves.

We interviewed managers and members of multicultural teams from all over the world. These interviews, combined with our deep research on dispute resolution and teamwork, led us to conclude that the wrong kind of managerial intervention may sideline valuable members who should be participating or, worse, create resistance, resulting in poor team performance. We're not talking here about respecting differing national standards for doing business, such as accounting practices. We're referring to day-to-day working problems among team members that can keep multicultural teams from realizing the very gains they were set up to harvest, such as knowledge of different product markets, culturally sensitive customer service, and 24-hour work rotations.

The good news is that cultural challenges are manageable if managers and team members choose the right strategy and avoid imposing single-culture-based approaches on multicultural situations.

The Challenges

People tend to assume that challenges on multicultural teams arise from differing styles of communication. But this is only one of the four categories that, according to our research, can create barriers to a team's ultimate success. These categories are direct versus indirect communication; trouble with accents and fluency; differing attitudes toward hierarchy and authority; and conflicting norms for decision making.

Direct versus indirect communication. Communication in Western cultures is typically direct and explicit. The meaning is on the surface, and a listener doesn't have to know much about the context or the speaker to interpret it. This is not true in many other cultures, where meaning is embedded in the way the message is presented. For example, Western negotiators get crucial information about the other party's preferences and priorities by asking direct questions, such as "Do you prefer option A or option B?" In cultures that use indirect communication, negotiators may have to infer preferences and priorities from changes—or the lack of them—in the other party's settlement proposal. In cross-cultural negotiations, the non-Westerner can understand the direct communications of the Westerner, but the Westerner has difficulty understanding the indirect communications of the non-Westerner.

An American manager who was leading a project to build an interface for a U.S. and Japanese customer-data system explained the problems her team was having this way: "In Japan, they want to talk and discuss. Then we take a break and they talk within the organization. They want to make sure that there's harmony in the rest of the organization. One of the hardest lessons for me was when I thought they were saying yes but they just meant 'I'm listening to you.'"

The differences between direct and indirect communication can cause serious damage to relationships when team projects run into problems. When the American manager quoted above discovered that several flaws in the system would significantly disrupt company operations, she pointed this out in an e-mail to her American boss and the Japanese team members. Her boss appreciated the direct warnings; her Japanese colleagues were embarrassed, because she had violated their norms for uncovering and discussing problems. Their reaction was to provide her with less access to the people and information she needed to monitor progress. They would probably have responded better if she had pointed out the problems indirectly—for example, by asking them what would happen if a certain part of the system was not functioning properly, even though she knew full well that it was malfunctioning and also what the implications were.

As our research indicates is so often true, communication challenges create barriers to effective teamwork by reducing information sharing, creating interpersonal conflict, or both. In Japan, a typical response to direct confrontation is to isolate the norm violator. This American manager was isolated not just socially but also physically. She told us, "They literally put my office in a storage room, where I had desks stacked from floor to ceiling and I was the only person there. So they totally isolated me, which was a pretty loud signal to me that I was not a part of the inside circle and that they would communicate with me only as needed."

Her direct approach had been intended to solve a problem, and in one sense, it did, because her project was launched problem-free. But her norm violations exacerbated the challenges of working with her Japanese colleagues and limited her ability to uncover any other problems that might have derailed the project later on.

Jeanne Brett is the DeWitt W. Buchanan, Jr., Distinguished Professor of Dispute Resolution and Organizations and the director of the Dispute Resolution Research Center at Northwestern University's Kellogg School of Management in Evanston, Illinois. **Kristin Behfar** is an assistant professor at the Paul Merage School of Business at the University of California at Irvine. **Mary C. Kern** is an assistant professor at the Zicklin School of Business at Baruch College in New York.

Trouble with accents and fluency. Although the language of international business is English, misunderstandings or deep frustration may occur because of nonnative speakers' accents, lack of fluency, or problems with translation or usage. These may also influence perceptions of status or competence.

For example, a Latin American member of a multicultural consulting team lamented, "Many times I felt that because of the language difference, I didn't have the words to say some things that I was thinking. I noticed that when I went to these interviews with the U.S. guy, he would tend to lead the interviews, which was understandable but also disappointing, because we are at the same level. I had very good questions, but he would take the lead."

When we interviewed an American member of a U.S.-Japanese team that was assessing the potential expansion of a U.S. retail chain into Japan, she described one American teammate this way: "He was not interested in the Japanese consultants' feedback and felt that because they weren't as fluent as he was, they weren't intelligent enough and, therefore, could add no value." The team member described was responsible for assessing one aspect of the feasibility of expansion into Japan. Without input from the Japanese experts, he risked overestimating opportunities and underestimating challenges.

Nonfluent team members may well be the most expert on the team, but their difficulty communicating knowledge makes it hard for the team to recognize and utilize their expertise. If teammates become frustrated or impatient with a lack of fluency, interpersonal conflicts can arise. Nonnative speakers may become less motivated to contribute, or anxious about their performance evaluations and future career prospects. The organization as a whole pays a greater price: Its investment in a multicultural team fails to pay off.

Some teams, we learned, use language differences to resolve (rather than create) tensions. A team of U.S. and Latin American buyers was negotiating with a team from a Korean supplier. The negotiations took place in Korea, but the discussions were conducted in English. Frequently the Koreans would caucus at the table by speaking Korean. The buyers, frustrated, would respond by appearing to caucus in Spanish—though they discussed only inconsequential current events and sports, in case any of the Koreans spoke Spanish. Members of the team who didn't speak Spanish pretended to participate, to the great amusement of their teammates. This approach proved effective: It conveyed to the Koreans in an appropriately indirect way that their caucuses in Korean were frustrating and annoying to the other side. As a result, both teams cut back on sidebar conversations.

Differing attitudes toward hierarchy and authority. A challenge inherent in multicultural teamwork is that by design, teams have a rather flat structure. But team members from some cultures, in which people are treated differently according to their status in an organization, are uncomfortable on flat teams. If they defer to higher-status team members, their behavior will be seen as appropriate when most of the team comes from a hierarchical culture; but they may damage their stature and credibility—and even face humiliation—if most of the team comes from an egalitarian culture.

One manager of Mexican heritage, who was working on a credit and underwriting team for a bank, told us, "In Mexican culture, you're always supposed to be humble. So whether you understand something or not, you're supposed to put it in the form of a question. You have to keep it open-ended, out of respect. I think that actually worked against me, because the Americans thought I really didn't know what I was talking about. So it made me feel like they thought I was wavering on my answer."

When, as a result of differing cultural norms, team members believe they've been treated disrespectfully, the whole project can blow up. In another Korean-U.S. negotiation, the American members of a due diligence team were having difficulty getting information from their Korean counterparts, so they complained directly to higher-level Korean management, nearly wrecking the deal. The higher-level managers were offended because hierarchy is strictly adhered to in Korean organizations and culture. It should have been their own lower-level people, not the U.S. team members, who came to them with a problem. And the Korean team members were mortified that their bosses had been involved before they themselves could brief them. The crisis was resolved only when high-

Team members who are uncomfortable on flat teams may, by deferring to higher-status teammates, damage their stature and credibility— and even face humiliation—if most of the team is from an egalitarian culture.

level U.S. managers made a trip to Korea, conveying appropriate respect for their Korean counterparts.

Conflicting norms for decision making. Cultures differ enormously when it comes to decision making—particularly, how quickly decisions should be made and how much analysis is required beforehand. Not surprisingly, U.S. managers like to make decisions very quickly and with relatively little analysis by comparison with managers from other countries.

A Brazilian manager at an American company who was negotiating to buy Korean products destined for Latin America told us, "On the first day, we agreed on three points, and on the second day, the U.S.-Spanish side wanted to start with point four. But the Korean side wanted to go back and rediscuss points one through three. My boss almost had an attack."

What U.S. team members learn from an experience like this is that the American way simply cannot be imposed on other cultures. Managers from other cultures may, for example, decline to share information until they understand the full scope of a project. But they have learned that they can't simply ignore the desire of their American counterparts to make decisions quickly. What to do? The best solution seems to be to make minor concessions on process—to learn to adjust to and even respect another approach to decision making. For example, American managers have learned to keep their impatient bosses away from team meetings and give them frequent if brief updates. A comparable lesson for managers from other cultures is to be explicit about what they need—saying, for example, "We have to see the big picture before we talk details."

Four Strategies

The most successful teams and managers we interviewed used four strategies for dealing with these challenges: adaptation (acknowledging cultural gaps openly and working around them), structural intervention (changing the shape of the team), managerial intervention (setting norms early or bringing in a higher-level manager), and exit (removing a team member when other options have failed). There is no one right way to deal with a particular kind of multicultural problem; identifying the type of challenge is only the

first step. The more crucial step is assessing the circumstances—or "enabling situational conditions"—under which the team is working. For example, does the project allow any flexibility for change, or do deadlines make that impossible? Are there additional resources available that might be tapped? Is the team permanent or temporary? Does the team's manager have the autonomy to make a decision about changing the team in some way? Once the situational conditions have been analyzed, the team's leader can identify an appropriate response (see the exhibit "Identifying the Right Strategy").

Adaptation. Some teams find ways to work with or around the challenges they face, adapting practices or attitudes without making changes to the group's membership or assignments. Adaptation works when team members are willing to acknowledge and name their cultural differences and to assume responsibility for figuring out how to live with them. It's often the best possible approach to a problem, because it typically involves less managerial time than other strategies; and because team members participate in solving the problem themselves, they learn from the process. When team members have this mind-set, they can be creative about protecting their own substantive differences while acceding to the processes of others.

An American software engineer located in Ireland who was working with an Israeli account management team from his own company told us how shocked he was by the Israelis' in-your-face style: "There were definitely different ways of approaching issues and discussing them. There is something pretty common to the Israeli culture: They like to argue. I tend to try to collaborate more, and it got very stressful for me until I figured out how to kind of merge the cultures."

The software engineer adapted. He imposed some structure on the Israelis that helped him maintain his own style of being thoroughly prepared; that accommodation enabled him to accept the Israeli style. He also noticed that team members weren't just confronting him; they confronted one another but were able to work together effectively nevertheless. He realized that the confrontation was not personal but cultural.

In another example, an American member of a postmerger consulting team was frustrated by the hierarchy of the French company his team was working with. He felt that a meeting with certain French managers who were not directly involved in the merger "wouldn't deliver any value to me or for purposes of the project," but said that he had come to understand that "it was very important to really involve all the people there" if the integration was ultimately to work.

A U.S. and UK multicultural team tried to use their differing approaches to decision making to reach a higher-quality decision. This approach, called fusion, is getting serious attention from political scientists and from government officials dealing with multicultural populations that want to protect their cultures rather than integrate or assimilate. If the team had relied exclusively on the Americans' "forge ahead" approach, it might not have recognized the pitfalls that lay ahead and might later have had to back up and start over. Meanwhile, the UK members would have been gritting their teeth and saying "We told you things were moving too fast." If the team had used the "Let's think about this" UK approach, it might have wasted a lot of time

Identifying the Right Strategy

The most successful teams and managers we interviewed use four strategies for dealing with problems: adaptation (acknowledging cultural gaps openly and working around them), structural intervention (changing the shape of the team), managerial intervention (setting norms early or bringing in a higher-level manager), and exit (removing a team member when other options have failed). Adaptation is the ideal strategy because the team works effectively to solve its own problem with minimal input from management—and, most important, learns from the experience. The guide below can help you identify the right strategy once you have identified both the problem and the "enabling situational conditions" that apply to the team.

REPRESENTATIVE PROBLEMS	ENABLING SITUATIONAL CONDITIONS	STRATEGY	COMPLICATING FACTORS
• Conflict arises from decision-making differences • Misunderstanding or stonewalling arises from communication differences	• Team members can attribute a challenge to culture rather than personality • Higher-level managers are not available or the team would be embarrassed to involve them	**Adaptation**	• Team members must be exceptionally aware • Negotiating a common understanding takes time
• The team is affected by emotional tensions relating to fluency issues or prejudice • Team members are inhibited by perceived status differences among teammates	• The team can be subdivided to mix cultures or expertise • Tasks can be subdivided	**Structural Intervention**	• If team members aren't carefully distributed, subgroups can strengthen preexisting differences • Subgroup solutions have to fit back together
• Violations of hierarchy have resulted in loss of face • An absence of ground rules is causing conflict	• The problem has produced a high level of emotion • The team has reached a stalemate • A higher-level manager is able and willing to intervene	**Managerial Intervention**	• The team becomes overly dependent on the manager • Team members may be sidelined or resistant
• A team member cannot adjust to the challenge at hand and has become unable to contribute to the project	• The team is permanent rather than temporary • Emotions are beyond the point of intervention • Too much face has been lost	**Exit**	• Talent and training costs are lost

trying to identify every pitfall, including the most unlikely, while the U.S. members chomped at the bit and muttered about analysis paralysis. The strength of this team was that some of its members were willing to forge ahead and some were willing to work through pitfalls. To accommodate them all, the team did both—moving not quite as fast as the U.S. members would have on their own and not quite as thoroughly as the UK members would have.

Structural intervention. A structural intervention is a deliberate reorganization or reassignment designed to reduce interpersonal friction or to remove a source of conflict for one or more groups. This approach can be extremely effective when obvious subgroups demarcate the team (for example, headquarters versus national subsidiaries) or if team members are proud, defensive, threatened, or clinging to negative stereotypes of one another.

A member of an investment research team scattered across continental Europe, the UK, and the U.S. described for us how his manager resolved conflicts stemming from status differences and language tensions among the team's three "tribes." The manager started by having the team meet face-to-face twice a year, not to discuss mundane day-to-day problems (of which there were many) but to identify a set of values that the team would use to direct and evaluate its progress. At the first meeting, he realized that when he started to speak, everyone else "shut down," waiting to hear what he had to say. So he hired a consultant to run future meetings. The consultant didn't represent a hierarchical threat and was therefore able to get lots of participation from team members.

Another structural intervention might be to create smaller working groups of mixed cultures or mixed corporate identities in order to get at information that is not forthcoming from the team as a whole. The manager of the team that was evaluating retail opportunities in Japan used this approach. When she realized that the female Japanese consultants would not participate if the group got large, or if their male superior was present, she broke the team up into smaller groups to try to solve problems. She used this technique repeatedly and made a point of changing the subgroups' membership each time so that team members got to know and respect everyone else on the team.

The subgrouping technique involves risks, however. It buffers people who are not working well together or not participating in the larger group for one reason or another. Sooner or later the team will have to assemble the pieces that the subgroups have come up with, so this approach relies on another structural intervention: Someone must become a mediator in order to see that the various pieces fit together.

Managerial intervention. When a manager behaves like an arbitrator or a judge, making a final decision without team involvement, neither the manager nor the team gains much insight into why the team has stalemated. But it is possible for team members to use managerial intervention effectively to sort out problems.

When an American refinery-safety expert with significant experience throughout East Asia got stymied during a project in China, she called in her company's higher-level managers in Beijing to talk to the higher-level managers to whom the Chinese refinery's managers reported. Unlike the Western team members who breached etiquette by approaching the superiors of their Korean counterparts, the safety expert made sure to respect hierarchies in both organizations.

"Trying to resolve the issues," she told us, "the local management at the Chinese refinery would end up having conferences with our Beijing office and also with the upper management within the refinery. Eventually they understood that we weren't trying to insult them or their culture or to tell them they were bad in any way. We were trying to help. They eventually understood that there were significant fire and safety issues. But we actually had to go up some levels of management to get those resolved."

Managerial intervention to set norms early in a team's life can really help the team start out with effective processes. In one instance reported to us, a multicultural software development team's lingua franca was English, but some members, though they spoke grammatically correct English, had a very pronounced accent. In setting the ground rules for the team, the manager addressed the challenge directly, telling the members that they had been chosen for their task expertise, not their fluency in English, and that the team was going to have to work around language problems. As the project moved to the customer-services training stage, the manager advised the team members to acknowledge their accents up front. She said they should tell customers, "I realize I have an accent. If you don't understand what I'm saying, just stop me and ask questions."

Exit. Possibly because many of the teams we studied were project based, we found that leaving the team was an infrequent strategy for managing challenges. In short-term situations, unhappy team members often just waited out the project. When teams were permanent, producing products or services, the exit of one or more members was a strategy of last resort, but it was used—either voluntarily or after a formal request from management. Exit was likely when emotions were running high and too much face had been lost on both sides to salvage the situation.

An American member of a multicultural consulting team described the conflict between two senior consultants, one a Greek woman and the other a Polish man, over how to approach problems: "The woman from Greece would say, 'Here's the way I think we should do it.' It would be something that she was in control of. The guy from Poland would say, 'I think we should actually do it this way instead.' The woman would kind of turn red in the face, upset, and say, 'I just don't think that's the right way of doing it.' It would definitely switch from just professional differences to personal differences.

"The woman from Greece ended up leaving the firm. That was a direct result of probably all the different issues going on between these people. It really just wasn't a good fit. I've found that oftentimes when you're in consulting, you have to adapt to the culture, obviously, but you have to adapt just as much to the style of whoever is leading the project."

• • •

Though multicultural teams face challenges that are not directly attributable to cultural differences, such differences underlay whatever problem needed to be addressed in many of the teams we studied. Furthermore, while serious in their own right when they have a negative effect on team functioning, cultural challenges may also unmask fundamental managerial problems. Managers who inter-

vene early and set norms; teams and managers who structure social interaction and work to engage everyone on the team; and teams that can see problems as stemming from culture, not personality, approach challenges with good humor and creativity. Managers who have to intervene when the team has reached a stalemate may be able to get the team moving again, but they seldom empower it to help itself the next time a stalemate occurs.

When frustrated team members take some time to think through challenges and possible solutions themselves, it can make a huge difference. Take, for example, this story about a financial-services call center. The members of the call-center team were all fluent Spanish-speakers, but some were North Americans and some were Latin Americans. Team performance, measured by calls answered per hour, was lagging. One Latin American was taking twice as long with her calls as the rest of the team. She was handling callers' questions appropriately, but she was also engaging in chitchat. When her teammates confronted her for being a free rider (they resented having to make up for her low call rate), she immediately acknowledged the problem, admitting that she did not know how to end the call politely—chitchat being normal in her culture. They rallied to help her: Using their technology, they would break into any of her calls that went overtime, excusing themselves to the customer, offering to take over the call, and saying that this employee was urgently needed to help out on a different call. The team's solution worked in the short run, and the employee got better at ending her calls in the long run.

In another case, the Indian manager of a multicultural team coordinating a company-wide IT project found himself frustrated when he and a teammate from Singapore met with two Japanese members of the coordinating team to try to get the Japan section to deliver its part of the project. The Japanese members seemed to be saying yes, but in the Indian manager's view, their follow-through was insufficient. He considered and rejected the idea of going up the hierarchy to the Japanese team members' boss, and decided instead to try to build consensus with the whole Japanese IT team, not just the two members on the coordinating team. He and his Singapore teammate put together an eBusiness

One team manager addressed the language challenge directly, telling the members that they had been chosen for their task expertise, not their fluency in English, and that the team would have to work around problems.

road show, took it to Japan, invited the whole IT team to view it at a lunch meeting, and walked through success stories about other parts of the organization that had aligned with the company's larger business priorities. It was rather subtle, he told us, but it worked. The Japanese IT team wanted to be spotlighted in future eBusiness road shows. In the end, the whole team worked well together— and no higher-level manager had to get involved.

Reprint R0611D
To order, see the next page
or call 800-988-0886 or 617-783-7500
or go to www.hbrreprints.org

Managing Multicultural Teams

Further Reading

ARTICLES

Making Differences Matter: A New Paradigm for Managing Diversity
by David A. Thomas and Robin J. Ely
Harvard Business Review
September 1996
Product no. 96510

You can strengthen your teams' ability to use the adaptation process suggested by Brett, Behfar, and Kern by fostering a working environment in which cultural differences are valued. To cultivate such an environment: 1) Encourage open discussion of cultural backgrounds. For instance, a food company's Chinese chemist draws on her cooking, not her scientific, experience to solve a soup-flavoring problem. 2) Eliminate forms of dominance—by hierarchy, function, race, gender, and so forth—that inhibit team members' full contribution. 3) Acknowledge and swiftly resolve the inevitable tensions that arise when employees from different backgrounds share ideas and emotions.

Oil and *Wasser*
by Byron Reimus
Harvard Business Review
May 2004
Product no. R0405X

In this fictional case study, executives from an English firm and a German company who are seeking a supposed "merger of equals" must resolve cross-cultural tensions threatening the deal. Four experts provide suggestions. For example, develop a new shared vision and common strategic goals for the project (such as "Beat the competition and become number one") that rise above national differences. Cultivate personal relationships with the "other" to eliminate stereotypes, by getting together in relaxed, shoptalk-free social settings. When you get to know one another as individuals, it becomes easier to let go of negative stereotypes.

Cultural Intelligence
by P. Christopher Earley and Elaine Mosakowski
Harvard Business Review
October 2004
Product no. R0410J

Team members can further strengthen their adaptation skills by developing their *cultural intelligence*. 1) Look for clues to the shared understandings that define another culture. For example, do people from that culture tend to be strict or flexible about deadlines? Are they receptive to highly imaginative ideas, or do they prefer more conservative thinking? 2) Adopt the habits and mannerisms of people from other cultures. You'll discover in an elemental way what it's like to be them. And you'll demonstrate respect for their ways. 3) Cultivate confidence that you can overcome multicultural obstacles and setbacks and that you're capable of understanding people from unfamiliar cultures.

Harvard Business Review

To Order

For *Harvard Business Review* reprints and subscriptions, call 800-988-0886 or 617-783-7500. Go to www.hbrreprints.org

For customized and quantity orders of *Harvard Business Review* article reprints, call 617-783-7626, or e-mail customizations@hbsp.harvard.edu

Harvard Business Review

www.hbrreprints.org

Great leaders tap into the needs and fears we all share. Great managers, by contrast, perform their magic by discovering, developing, and celebrating what's different about each person who works for them. Here's how they do it.

What Great Managers Do

by Marcus Buckingham

Included with this full-text *Harvard Business Review* article:

Reprint R0503D

What Great Managers Do

The Idea in Brief

You've spent months coaching that employee to treat customers better, work more independently, or get organized—all to no avail.

How to make better use of your precious time? Do what great managers do: Instead of trying to change your employees, identify their unique abilities (and even their eccentricities)—then help them use those qualities to excel in their own way.

You'll need these three tactics:

- **Continuously tweak roles to capitalize on individual strengths.** One Walgreens store manager put a laconic but highly organized employee in charge of restocking aisles—freeing up more sociable employees to serve customers.

- **Pull the triggers that activate employees' strengths.** Offer incentives such as time spent with you, opportunities to work independently, and recognition in forms each employee values most.

- **Tailor coaching to unique learning styles.** Give "analyzers" the information they need before starting a task. Start "doers" off with simple tasks, then gradually raise the bar. Let "watchers" ride shotgun with your most experienced performers.

The payoff for capitalizing on employees' unique strengths? You save time. Your people take ownership for improving their skills. And you teach employees to value differences—building a powerful sense of team.

The Idea in Practice

A closer look at the three tactics:

CAPITALIZE ON EMPLOYEES' STRENGTHS

First identify each employee's unique strengths: Walk around, observing people's reactions to events. Note activities each employee is drawn to. Ask "What was the best day at work you've had in the past three months?" Listen for activities people find intrinsically satisfying.

Watch for weaknesses, too, but downplay them in your communications with employees. Offer training to help employees overcome shortcomings stemming from lack of skills or knowledge. Otherwise, apply these strategies:

- **Find the employee a partner with complementary talents.** A merchandising manager who couldn't start tasks without exhaustive information performed superbly once her supervisor (the VP) began acting as her "information partner." The VP committed to leaving the manager a brief voicemail update daily and arranging two "touch base" conversations weekly.

- **Reconfigure work to neutralize weaknesses.** Use your creativity to envision more effective work arrangements, and be courageous about adopting unconventional job designs.

ACTIVATE EMPLOYEES' STRENGTHS

The ultimate trigger for activating an employee's strengths is recognition. But each employee plays to a different audience. So tailor your praise accordingly.

IF AN EMPLOYEE VALUES RECOGNITION FROM...	PRAISE HIM BY...
His peers	Publicly celebrating his achievement in front of coworkers
You	Telling him privately but vividly why he's such a valuable team member
Others with similar expertise	Giving him a professional or technical award
Customers	Posting a photo of him and his best customer in the office

TAILOR COACHING TO LEARNING STYLE

Adapt your coaching efforts to each employee's unique learning style:

IF AN EMPLOYEE IS...	COACH HIM BY...
An **"analyzer"**—he requires extensive information before taking on a task, and he hates making mistakes	• Giving him ample classroom time • Role-playing with him • Giving him time to prepare for challenges
A **"doer"**—he uses trial and error to enhance his skills while grappling with tasks	• Assigning him a simple task, explaining the desired outcomes, and getting out of his way • Gradually increasing a task's complexity until he masters his role
A **"watcher"**—he hones his skills by watching other people in action	• Having him "shadow" top performers.

Great leaders tap into the needs and fears we all share. Great managers, by contrast, perform their magic by discovering, developing, and celebrating what's different about each person who works for them. Here's how they do it.

What Great Managers Do

by Marcus Buckingham

"The best boss I ever had." That's a phrase most of us have said or heard at some point, but what does it mean? What sets the great boss apart from the average boss? The literature is rife with provocative writing about the qualities of managers and leaders and whether the two differ, but little has been said about what happens in the thousands of daily interactions and decisions that allows managers to get the best out of their people and win their devotion. What do great managers actually *do*?

In my research, beginning with a survey of 80,000 managers conducted by the Gallup Organization and continuing during the past two years with in-depth studies of a few top performers, I've found that while there are as many styles of management as there are managers, there is one quality that sets truly great managers apart from the rest: They discover what is unique about each person and then capitalize on it. Average managers play checkers, while great managers play chess. The difference? In checkers, all the pieces

are uniform and move in the same way; they are interchangeable. You need to plan and coordinate their movements, certainly, but they all move at the same pace, on parallel paths. In chess, each type of piece moves in a different way, and you can't play if you don't know how each piece moves. More important, you won't win if you don't think carefully about how you move the pieces. Great managers know and value the unique abilities and even the eccentricities of their employees, and they learn how best to integrate them into a coordinated plan of attack.

This is the exact opposite of what great leaders do. Great leaders discover what is universal and capitalize on it. Their job is to rally people toward a better future. Leaders can succeed in this only when they can cut through differences of race, sex, age, nationality, and personality and, using stories and celebrating heroes, tap into those very few needs we all share. The job of a manager, meanwhile, is to turn one person's particular talent into performance. Managers will succeed only when they can identify and deploy the differences among people, challenging each employee to excel in his or her own way. This doesn't mean a leader can't be a manager or vice versa. But to excel at one or both, you must be aware of the very different skills each role requires.

The Game of Chess

What does the chess game look like in action? When I visited Michelle Miller, the manager who opened Walgreens' 4,000th store, I found the wall of her back office papered with work schedules. Michelle's store in Redondo Beach, California, employs people with sharply different skills and potentially disruptive differences in personality. A critical part of her job, therefore, is to put people into roles and shifts that will allow them to shine—and to avoid putting clashing personalities together. At the same time, she needs to find ways for individuals to grow.

There's Jeffrey, for example, a "goth rocker" whose hair is shaved on one side and long enough on the other side to cover his face. Michelle almost didn't hire him because he couldn't quite look her in the eye during his interview, but he wanted the hard-to-cover night shift, so she decided to give him a chance. After a couple of months, she noticed that when she gave Jeffrey a vague assignment, such as "Straighten up the merchandise in every aisle," what should have been a two-hour job would take him all night—and wouldn't be done very well. But if she gave him a more specific task, such as "Put up all the risers for Christmas," all the risers would be symmetrical, with the right merchandise on each one, perfectly priced, labeled, and "faced" (turned toward the customer). Give Jeffrey a generic task, and he would struggle. Give him one that forced him to be accurate and analytical, and he would excel. This, Michelle concluded, was Jeffrey's forte. So, as any good manager would do, she told him what she had deduced about him and praised him for his good work.

And a good manager would have left it at that. But Michelle knew she could get more out of Jeffrey. So she devised a scheme to reassign responsibilities across the entire store to capitalize on his unique strengths. In every Walgreens, there is a responsibility called "resets and revisions." A reset involves stocking an aisle with new merchandise, a task that usually coincides with a predictable change in cus-

tomer buying patterns (at the end of summer, for example, the stores will replace sun creams and lip balms with allergy medicines). A revision is a less time-consuming but more frequent version of the same thing: Replace these cartons of toothpaste with this new and improved variety. Display this new line of detergent at this end of the row. Each aisle requires some form of revision at least once a week.

In most Walgreens stores, each employee "owns" one aisle, where she is responsible not only for serving customers but also for facing the merchandise, keeping the aisle clean and orderly, tagging items with a Telxon gun, and conducting all resets and revisions. This arrangement is simple and efficient, and it affords each employee a sense of personal responsibility. But Michelle decided that since Jeffrey was so good at resets and revisions—and didn't enjoy interacting with customers—this should be his full-time job, in every single aisle.

It was a challenge. One week's worth of revisions requires a binder three inches thick. But Michelle reasoned that not only would Jeffrey be excited by the challenge and get better and better with practice, but other employees would be freed from what they considered a chore and have more time to greet and serve customers. The store's performance proved her right. After the reorganization, Michelle saw not only increases in sales and profit but also in that most critical performance metric, customer satisfaction. In the subsequent four months, her store netted perfect scores in Walgreens' mystery shopper program.

So far, so very good. Sadly, it didn't last. This "perfect" arrangement depended on Jeffrey remaining content, and he didn't. With his success at doing resets and revisions, his confidence grew, and six months into the job, he wanted to move into management. Michelle wasn't disappointed by this, however; she was intrigued. She had watched Jeffrey's progress closely and had already decided that he might do well as a manager, though he wouldn't be a particularly emotive one. Besides, like any good chess player, she had been thinking a couple of moves ahead.

Over in the cosmetics aisle worked an employee named Genoa. Michelle saw Genoa as something of a double threat. Not only was she adept at putting customers at ease—she remembered their names, asked good questions,

Marcus Buckingham (info@ onethinginc.com) is a consultant and speaker on leadership and management practices. He is the coauthor of *First, Break All the Rules* (Simon & Schuster, 1999) and *Now, Discover Your Strengths* (Free Press, 2001). This article is copyright 2005 by One Thing Productions and has been adapted with permission from Buckingham's new book, *The One Thing You Need to Know* (Free Press, March 2005).

was welcoming yet professional when answering the phone—but she was also a neatnik. The cosmetics department was always perfectly faced, every product remained aligned, and everything was arranged just so. Her aisle was sexy: It made you want to reach out and touch the merchandise.

To capitalize on these twin talents, and to accommodate Jeffrey's desire for promotion, Michelle shuffled the roles within the store once again. She split Jeffrey's reset and revision job in two and gave the "revision" part of it to Genoa so that the whole store could now benefit from her ability to arrange merchandise attractively. But Michelle didn't want the store to miss out on Genoa's gift for customer service, so Michelle asked her to focus on the revision role only between 8:30 AM and 11 AM, and after that, when the store began to fill with customers on their lunch breaks, Genoa should shift her focus over to them.

She kept the reset role with Jeffrey. Assistant managers don't usually have an ongoing responsibility in the store, but, Michelle reasoned, he was now so good and so fast at tearing an aisle apart and rebuilding it that he could easily finish a major reset during a five-hour stint, so he could handle resets along with his managerial responsibilities.

By the time you read this, the Jeffrey–Genoa configuration has probably outlived its usefulness, and Michelle has moved on to design other effective and inventive configurations. The ability to keep tweaking roles to capitalize on the uniqueness of each person is the essence of great management.

A manager's approach to capitalizing on differences can vary tremendously from place to place. Walk into the back office at another Walgreens, this one in San Jose, California, managed by Jim Kawashima, and you won't see a single work schedule. Instead, the walls are covered with sales figures and statistics, the best of them circled with red felt-tip pen, and dozens of photographs of sales contest winners, most featuring a customer service representative named Manjit.

Manjit outperforms her peers consistently. When I first heard about her, she had just won a competition in Walgreens' suggestive selling program to sell the most units of Gillette deodorant in a month. The national average was 300; Manjit had sold 1,600. Disposable cameras, toothpaste, batteries—you name it, she could sell it. And Manjit won contest after contest despite working the graveyard shift, from 12:30 AM to 8:30 AM, during which she met significantly fewer customers than did her peers.

Manjit hadn't always been such an exceptional performer. She became stunningly suc-

The Research

To gather the raw material for my book *The One Thing You Need to Know: About Great Managing, Great Leading, and Sustained Individual Success,* from which this article has been adapted, I chose an approach that is rather different from the one I used for my previous books. For 17 years, I had the good fortune to work with the Gallup Organization, one of the most respected research firms in the world. During that time, I was given the opportunity to interview some of the world's best leaders, managers, teachers, salespeople, stockbrokers, lawyers, and public servants. These interviews were a part of large-scale studies that involved surveying groups of people in the hopes of finding broad patterns in the data. For my book, I used this foundation as the jumping-off point for deeper, more individualized research.

In each of the three areas targeted in the book—managing, leading, and sustained individual success—I first identified one or two people in various roles and fields who had measurably, consistently, and dramatically outperformed their peers. These individuals included Myrtle Potter, president of commercial operations for Genentech, who transformed a failing drug into the highest selling prescription drug in the world; Sir Terry Leahy, the president of the European retailing giant Tesco; Manjit, the customer service representative from Jim Kawashima's top-performing Walgreens store in San Jose, California, who sold more than 1,600 units of Gillette deodorant in one month; and David Koepp, the prolific screenwriter who penned such blockbusters as *Jurassic Park, Mission: Impossible,* and *Spider-Man.*

What interested me about these high achievers was the practical, seemingly banal details of their actions and their choices. Why did Myrtle Potter repeatedly turn down promotions before taking on the challenge of turning around that failing drug? Why did Terry Leahy rely more on the memories of his working-class upbringing to define his company's strategy than on the results of customer surveys or focus groups? Manjit works the night shift, and one of her hobbies is weight lifting. Are those factors relevant to her performance? What were these special people doing that made them so very good at their roles?

Once these many details were duly noted and recorded, they slowly came together to reveal the "one thing" at the core of great managing, great leading, and sustained individual success.

cessful only when Jim, who has made a habit of resuscitating troubled stores, came on board. What did Jim do to initiate the change in Manjit? He quickly picked up on her idiosyncrasies and figured out how to translate them into outstanding performance. For example, back in India, Manjit was an athlete—a runner and a weight lifter—and had always thrilled to the challenge of measured performance. When I interviewed her, one of the first things out of her mouth was, "On Saturday, I sold 343 low-carb candy bars. On Sunday, I sold 367. Yesterday, 110, and today, 105." I asked if she always knows how well she's doing. "Oh yes," she replied. "Every day I check Mr. K's charts. Even on my day off, I make a point to come in and check my numbers."

Manjit loves to win and revels in public recognition. Hence, Jim's walls are covered with charts and figures, Manjit's scores are always highlighted in red, and there are photos documenting her success. Another manager might have asked Manjit to curb her enthusiasm for the limelight and give someone else a chance. Jim found a way to capitalize on it.

But what about Jim's other staff members? Instead of being resentful of Manjit's public recognition, the other employees came to understand that Jim took the time to see them as individuals and evaluate them based on their personal strengths. They also knew that Manjit's success spoke well of the entire store, so her success galvanized the team. In fact, before long, the pictures of Manjit began to include other employees from the store, too. After a few months, the San Jose location was ranked number one out of 4,000 in Walgreens' suggestive selling program.

Great Managers Are Romantics

Think back to Michelle. Her creative choreography may sound like a last resort, an attempt to make the best of a bad hire. It's not. Jeffrey and Genoa are not mediocre employees, and capitalizing on each person's uniqueness is a tremendously powerful tool.

First, identifying and capitalizing on each person's uniqueness saves time. No employee, however talented, is perfectly well-rounded. Michelle could have spent untold hours coaching Jeffrey and cajoling him into smiling at, making friends with, and remembering the names of customers, but she probably would have seen little result for her efforts. Her time was much better spent carving out a role that took advantage of Jeffrey's natural abilities.

Second, capitalizing on uniqueness makes each person more accountable. Michelle didn't just praise Jeffrey for his ability to execute specific assignments. She challenged him to make this ability the cornerstone of his contribution to the store, to take ownership for this ability, to practice it, and to refine it.

Third, capitalizing on what is unique about each person builds a stronger sense of team, because it creates interdependency. It helps

The Elusive "One Thing"

It's bold to characterize anything as *the* explanation or solution, so it's a risky move to make such definitive assertions as "this is the one thing all great managers do." But with enough research and focus, it is possible to identify that elusive "one thing."

I like to think of the concept of "one thing" as a "controlling insight." Controlling insights don't explain all outcomes or events; they serve as the best explanation of the greatest number of events. Such insights help you know which of your actions will have the most far-reaching influence in virtually every situation.

For a concept to emerge as the single controlling insight, it must pass three tests. First, it must be applicable across a wide range of situations. Take leadership as an example. Lately, much has been made of the notion that there is no one best way to lead and that instead, the most effective leadership style depends on the circumstance. While there is no doubt that different situations require different actions from a leader, that doesn't mean the most insightful thing you can say about leadership is that it's situational. With enough focus, you can identify the one thing that underpins successful leadership across all situations and all styles.

Second, a controlling insight must serve as a multiplier. In any equation, some factors will have only an additive value: When you focus your actions on these factors, you see some incremental improvement. The controlling insight should be more powerful. It should show you how to get exponential improvement. For example, good managing is the result of a combination of many actions—selecting talented employees, setting clear expectations, catching people doing things right, and so on—but none of these factors qualifies as the "one thing" that great managers do, because even when done well, these actions merely prevent managers from chasing their best employees away.

Finally, the controlling insight must guide action. It must point to precise things that can be done to create better outcomes more consistently. Insights that managers can act on—rather than simply ruminate over—are the ones that can make all the difference.

people appreciate one anothers' particular skills and learn that their coworkers can fill in where they are lacking. In short, it makes people need one another. The old cliché is that there's no "I" in "team." But as Michael Jordan once said, "There may be no 'I' in 'team,' but there is in 'win.'"

Finally, when you capitalize on what is unique about each person, you introduce a healthy degree of disruption into your world. You shuffle existing hierarchies: If Jeffrey is in charge of all resets and revisions in the store, should he now command more or less respect than an assistant manager? You also shuffle existing assumptions about who is allowed to do what: If Jeffrey devises new methods of resetting an aisle, does he have to ask permission to try these out, or can he experiment on his own? And you shuffle existing beliefs about where the true expertise lies: If Genoa comes up with a way of arranging new merchandise that she thinks is more appealing than the method suggested by the "planogram" sent down from Walgreens headquarters, does her expertise trump the planners back at corporate? These questions will challenge Walgreens' orthodoxies and thus will help the company become more inquisitive, more intelligent, more vital, and, despite its size, more able to duck and weave into the future.

All that said, the reason great managers focus on uniqueness isn't just because it makes good business sense. They do it because they can't help it. Like Shelley and Keats, the nineteenth-century Romantic poets, great managers are fascinated with individuality for its own sake. Fine shadings of personality, though they may be invisible to some and frustrating to others, are crystal clear to and highly valued by great managers. They could no more ignore these subtleties than ignore their own needs and desires. Figuring out what makes people tick is simply in their nature.

The Three Levers

Although the Romantics were mesmerized by differences, at some point, managers need to rein in their inquisitiveness, gather up what they know about a person, and put the employee's idiosyncrasies to use. To that end, there are three things you must know about someone to manage her well: her strengths, the triggers that activate those strengths, and how she learns.

Make the most of strengths. It takes time and effort to gain a full appreciation of an employee's strengths and weaknesses. The great manager spends a good deal of time outside the office walking around, watching each person's reactions to events, listening, and taking mental notes about what each individual is drawn to and what each person struggles with. There's no substitute for this kind of observation, but you can obtain a lot of information about a person by asking a few simple, open-ended questions and listening carefully to the answers. Two queries in particular have proven most revealing when it comes to identifying strengths and weaknesses, and I recommend asking them of all new hires—and revisiting the questions periodically.

To identify a person's strengths, first ask, "What was the best day at work you've had in the past three months?" Find out what the person was doing and why he enjoyed it so much. Remember: A strength is not merely something you are good at. In fact, it might be something you aren't good at yet. It might be just a predilection, something you find so intrinsically satisfying that you look forward to doing it again and again and getting better at it over time. This question will prompt your employee to start thinking about his interests and abilities from this perspective.

To identify a person's weaknesses, just invert the question: "What was the worst day you've had at work in the past three months?" And then probe for details about what he was doing and why it grated on him so much. As with a strength, a weakness is not merely something you are bad at (in fact, you might be quite competent at it). It is something that drains you of energy, an activity that you never

What You Need to Know About Each of Your Direct Reports

☐ What are his or her strengths?

☐ What are the triggers that activate those strengths?

☐ What is his or her learning style?

look forward to doing and that when you are doing it, all you can think about is stopping.

Although you're keeping an eye out for both the strengths and weaknesses of your employees, your focus should be on their strengths. Conventional wisdom holds that self-awareness is a good thing and that it's the job of the manager to identify weaknesses and create a plan for overcoming them. But research by Albert Bandura, the father of social learning theory, has shown that self-assurance (labeled "self-efficacy" by cognitive psychologists), not self-awareness, is the strongest predictor of a person's ability to set high goals, to persist in the face of obstacles, to bounce back when reversals occur, and, ultimately, to achieve the goals they set. By contrast, self-awareness has not been shown to be a predictor of any of these outcomes, and in some cases, it appears to retard them.

Great managers seem to understand this instinctively. They know that their job is not to arm each employee with a dispassionately accurate understanding of the limits of her strengths and the liabilities of her weaknesses but to reinforce her self-assurance. That's why great managers focus on strengths. When a person succeeds, the great manager doesn't praise her hard work. Even if there's some exaggeration in the statement, he tells her that she succeeded because she has become so good at deploying her specific strengths. This, the manager knows, will strengthen the employee's self-assurance and make her more optimistic and more resilient in the face of challenges to come.

The focus-on-strengths approach might create in the employee a modicum of overconfidence, but great managers mitigate this by emphasizing the size and the difficulty of the employee's goals. They know that their primary objective is to create in each employee a specific state of mind: one that includes a realistic assessment of the difficulty of the obstacle ahead but an unrealistically optimistic belief in her ability to overcome it.

And what if the employee fails? Assuming the failure is not attributable to factors beyond her control, always explain failure as a lack of effort, even if this is only partially accurate. This will obscure self-doubt and give her something to work on as she faces up to the next challenge.

Repeated failure, of course, may indicate

Fine shadings of personality, though they may be invisible to some and frustrating to others, are crystal clear to and highly valued by great managers.

weakness where a role requires strength. In such cases, there are four approaches for overcoming weaknesses. If the problem amounts to a lack of skill or knowledge, that's easy to solve: Simply offer the relevant training, allow some time for the employee to incorporate the new skills, and look for signs of improvement. If her performance doesn't get better, you'll know that the reason she's struggling is because she is missing certain talents, a deficit no amount of skill or knowledge training is likely to fix. You'll have to find a way to manage around this weakness and neutralize it.

Which brings us to the second strategy for overcoming an employee weakness. Can you find her a partner, someone whose talents are strong in precisely the areas where hers are weak? Here's how this strategy can look in action. As vice president of merchandising for the women's clothing retailer Ann Taylor, Judi Langley found that tensions were rising between her and one of her merchandising managers, Claudia (not her real name), whose analytical mind and intense nature created an overpowering "need to know." If Claudia learned of something before Judi had a chance to review it with her, she would become deeply frustrated. Given the speed with which decisions were made, and given Judi's busy schedule, this happened frequently. Judi was concerned that Claudia's irritation was unsettling the whole product team, not to mention earning the employee a reputation as a malcontent.

An average manager might have identified this behavior as a weakness and lectured Claudia on how to control her need for information. Judi, however, realized that this "weakness" was an aspect of Claudia's greatest strength: her analytical mind. Claudia would never be able to rein it in, at least not for long. So Judi looked for a strategy that would honor and support Claudia's need to know, while channeling it more productively. Judi decided to act as Claudia's information partner, and she committed to leaving Claudia a voice mail at the end of each day with a brief update. To make sure nothing fell through the cracks, they set up two live "touch base" conversations per week. This solution managed Claudia's expectations and assured her that she would get the information she needed, if not exactly when she wanted it, then at least at frequent and predictable intervals. Giving Claudia a partner neutralized the negative manifestations of her strength, allowing her to focus her analytical mind on her work. (Of course, in most cases, the partner would need to be someone other than a manager.)

Should the perfect partner prove hard to find, try this third strategy: Insert into the employee's world a technique that helps accomplish through discipline what the person can't accomplish through instinct. I met one very successful screenwriter and director who had struggled with telling other professionals, such as composers and directors of photography, that their work was not up to snuff. So he devised a mental trick: He now imagines what the "god of art" would want and uses this imaginary entity as a source of strength. In his mind, he no longer imposes his own opinion on his colleagues but rather tells himself (and them) that an authoritative third party has weighed in.

If training produces no improvement, if complementary partnering proves impractical, and if no nifty discipline technique can be found, you are going to have to try the fourth and final strategy, which is to rearrange the employee's working world to render his weakness irrelevant, as Michelle Miller did with Jeffrey. This strategy will require of you, first, the creativity to envision a more effective arrangement and, second, the courage to make that arrangement work. But as Michelle's experience revealed, the payoff that may come in the form of increased employee productivity and engagement is well worth it.

Trigger good performance. A person's strengths aren't always on display. Sometimes they require precise triggering to turn them on. Squeeze the right trigger, and a person will push himself harder and persevere in the face of resistance. Squeeze the wrong one, and the person may well shut down. This can be tricky because triggers come in myriad and mysterious forms. One employee's trigger might be tied to the time of day (he is a night owl, and his strengths only kick in after 3 PM). Another employee's trigger might be tied to time with you, the boss (even though he's worked with you for more than five years, he still needs you to check in with him every day, or he feels he's being ignored). Another worker's trigger might be just the opposite—independence (she's only worked for you for six months, but if you check in with her even once a week, she feels micromanaged).

The most powerful trigger by far is recognition, not money. If you're not convinced of this, start ignoring one of your highly paid stars, and watch what happens. Most managers are aware that employees respond well to recognition. Great managers refine and extend this insight. They realize that each employee plays to a slightly different audience. To excel as a manager, you must be able to match the employee to the audience he values most. One employee's audience might be his peers; the best way to praise him would be to stand him up in front of his coworkers and publicly celebrate his achievement. Another's favorite audience might be you; the most powerful recognition would be a one-on-one conversation where you tell him quietly but vividly why he is such a valuable member of the team. Still another employee might define himself by his expertise; his most prized form of recognition would be some type of professional or technical award. Yet another might value feedback only from customers, in which case a picture of the employee with her best customer or a letter to her from the customer would be the best form of recognition.

Given how much personal attention it requires, tailoring praise to fit the person is mostly a manager's responsibility. But organizations can take a cue from this, too. There's no reason why a large company can't take this individualized approach to recognition and apply it to every employee. Of all the companies I've encountered, the North American division of HSBC, a London-based bank, has done the best job of this. Each year it presents its top individual consumer-lending performers with its Dream Awards. Each winner receives a unique prize. During the year, managers ask employees to identify what they would like to receive should they win. The prize value is capped at $10,000, and it cannot be redeemed as cash, but beyond those two restrictions, each employee is free to pick the prize he wants. At the end of the year, the company holds a Dream Awards gala, during which it shows a video about the winning employee and why he selected his particular prize.

You can imagine the impact these personalized prizes have on HSBC employees. It's one thing to be brought up on stage and given yet another plaque. It's another thing when, in addition to public recognition of your performance, you receive a college tuition fund for your child, or the Harley-Davidson motorcycle you've always dreamed of, or—the prize everyone at the company still talks about—the airline tickets to fly you and your family back to Mexico to visit the grandmother you haven't seen in ten years.

Tailor to learning styles. Although there are many learning styles, a careful review of adult learning theory reveals that three styles predominate. These three are not mutually exclusive; certain employees may rely on a combination of two or perhaps all three. Nonetheless, staying attuned to each employee's style or styles will help focus your coaching.

First, there's analyzing. Claudia from Ann Taylor is an analyzer. She understands a task by taking it apart, examining its elements, and reconstructing it piece by piece. Because every single component of a task is important in her eyes, she craves information. She needs to absorb all there is to know about a subject before she can begin to feel comfortable with it. If she doesn't feel she has enough information, she will dig and push until she gets it. She will read the assigned reading. She will attend the required classes. She will take good notes. She will study. And she will still want more.

The best way to teach an analyzer is to give her ample time in the classroom. Role-play with her. Do postmortem exercises with her. Break her performance down into its component parts so she can carefully build it back up. Always allow her time to prepare. The analyzer hates mistakes. A commonly held view is that mistakes fuel learning, but for the analyzer, this just isn't true. In fact, the reason she prepares so diligently is to minimize the possibility of mistakes. So don't expect to teach her much by throwing her into a new situation and telling her to wing it.

The opposite is true for the second dominant learning style, doing. While the most powerful learning moments for the analyzer occur prior to the performance, the doer's most powerful moments occur *during* the performance. Trial and error are integral to this learning process. Jeffrey, from Michelle Miller's store, is a doer. He learns the most while he's in the act of figuring things out for himself. For him, preparation is a dry, uninspiring activity. So rather than role-play with someone like Jeffrey, pick a specific task within his role that is simple but real, give him a brief overview of the outcomes you want, and get

out of his way. Then gradually increase the degree of each task's complexity until he has mastered every aspect of his role. He may make a few mistakes along the way, but for the doer, mistakes are the raw material for learning.

Finally, there's watching. Watchers won't learn much through role-playing. They won't learn by doing, either. Since most formal training programs incorporate both of these elements, watchers are often viewed as rather poor students. That may be true, but they aren't necessarily poor learners.

Watchers can learn a great deal when they are given the chance to see the total performance. Studying the individual parts of a task is about as meaningful for them as studying the individual pixels of a digital photograph. What's important for this type of learner is the content of each pixel, its position relative to all the others. Watchers are only able to see this when they view the complete picture.

As it happens, this is the way I learn. Years ago, when I first began interviewing, I struggled to learn the skill of creating a report on a person after I had interviewed him. I understood all the required steps, but I couldn't seem to put them together. Some of my colleagues could knock out a report in an hour; for me, it would take the better part of a day. Then one afternoon, as I was staring morosely into my Dictaphone, I overheard the voice of the analyst next door. He was talking so rapidly that I initially thought he was on the phone. Only after a few minutes did I realize that he was dictating a report. This was the first time I had heard someone "in the act." I'd seen the finished results countless times, since reading the reports of others was the way we were supposed to learn, but I'd never actually heard another analyst in the act of creation. It was a revelation. I finally saw how everything should come together into a coherent whole. I remember picking up my Dictaphone, mimicking the cadence and even the accent of my neighbor, and feeling the words begin to flow.

If you're trying to teach a watcher, by far the most effective technique is to get her out of the classroom. Take her away from the manuals, and make her ride shotgun with one of your most experienced performers.

• • •

We've seen, in the stories of great managers like Michelle Miller and Judi Langley, that at the very heart of their success lies an appreciation for individuality. This is not to say that managers don't need other skills. They need to be able to hire well, to set expectations, and to interact productively with their own bosses, just to name a few. But what they do—instinctively—is play chess. Mediocre managers assume (or hope) that their employees will all be motivated by the same things and driven by the same goals, that they will desire the same kinds of relationships and learn in roughly the same way. They define the behaviors they expect from people and tell them to work on behaviors that don't come naturally. They praise those who can overcome their natural styles to conform to preset ideas. In short, they believe the manager's job is to mold, or transform, each employee into the perfect version of the role.

Great managers don't try to change a person's style. They never try to push a knight to move in the same way as a bishop. They know that their employees will differ in how they think, how they build relationships, how altruistic they are, how patient they can be, how much of an expert they need to be, how prepared they need to feel, what drives them, what challenges them, and what their goals are. These differences of trait and talent are like blood types: They cut across the superficial variations of race, sex, and age and capture the essential uniqueness of each individual.

Like blood types, the majority of these differences are enduring and resistant to change. A manager's most precious resource is time, and great managers know that the most effective way to invest their time is to identify exactly how each employee is different and then to figure out how best to incorporate those enduring idiosyncrasies into the overall plan.

To excel at managing others, you must bring that insight to your actions and interactions. Always remember that great managing is about release, not transformation. It's about constantly tweaking your environment so that the unique contribution, the unique needs, and the unique style of each employee can be given free rein. Your success as a manager will depend almost entirely on your ability to do this.

Reprint R0503D
To order, see the next page
or call 800 988 0886 or 617 783 7500
or go to www.hbrreprints.org

Differences of trait and talent are like blood types: They cut across the superficial variations of race, sex, and age and capture each person's uniqueness.

What Great Managers Do

Further Reading

ARTICLES

How to Motivate Your Problem People
by Nigel Nicholson
Harvard Business Review
January 2003
Product no. R0301D

Nicholson provides additional guidelines for identifying the activities your people find intrinsically satisfying and unleashing employees' internal drive: 1) Through informal conversations, discern what drives an employee, what's blocking those drives, and what could happen if blockages were removed. 2) Consider how you or the organizational situation (a tough restructuring, for example) might be inadvertently blocking the person's motivation. 3) Affirm the employee's value to your company. 4) Test hunches about ways to co-opt the person's passion for productive ends. One manager found that a talented but reticent and angry employee was strongly motivated by his peers' respect. The manager asked him to consider becoming an adviser and technical coach for his unit—then asked him for ideas on how the new arrangement might work.

One More Time: How Do You Motivate Employees?
by Frederick Herzberg
Harvard Business Review
January 2003
Product no. R0301F

In this classic article, originally published in 1968, Herzberg focuses on the importance of tweaking job roles to capitalize on individual employees' strengths. To boost motivation, consider giving people responsibility for a complete process or unit of work. Enable people to take on new, more difficult tasks they haven't handled before. And assign individuals specialized tasks that allow them to become experts. Your reward? You'll have more time to spend on your *real* job: developing your staff rather than simply checking their work. Rather than trying to recharge your people's batteries again and again, you'll enable them to activate their own internal generators. Your employees' enthusiasm and commitment will rise—along with your company's overall performance.

Managing Away Bad Habits
by James Waldroop and Timothy Butler
Harvard Business Review
September–October 2000
Product no. R00512

Waldroop and Butler further examine strategies for helping employees overcome weaknesses that can't be addressed through skills training. The authors identify common "bad habits" and offer antidotes. For example, with "Heroes"—employees who drive themselves too hard and focus too much on the short term—point out the costs of burnout and encourage them to assess themselves for symptoms of overload. For "Bulldozers"—those who run roughshod over others but who get a lot done—point out how many enemies they've made and role-play conciliatory conversations with their victims. For "Pessimists"—people who emphasize the downside of change—teach them to objectively evaluate the pros and cons of proposed ideas *and* the risks of doing nothing.

Harvard Business Review

To Order

For *Harvard Business Review* reprints and subscriptions, call 800-988-0886 or 617-783-7500. Go to www.hbrreprints.org

For customized and quantity orders of *Harvard Business Review* article reprints, call 617-783-7626, or e-mail customizations@hbsp.harvard.edu